Some of the Words Are Theirs

The Art of Writing and Living a Sermon

Austin Carty

WILLIAM B. EERDMANS PUBLISHING COMPANY

GRAND RAPIDS, MICHIGAN

Wm. B. Eerdmans Publishing Co.
2006 44th Street SE, Grand Rapids, MI 49508
www.eerdmans.com

© 2025 Austin Carty
All rights reserved
Published 2025

Illustrations by Crystal Vandiver

Printed in the United States of America

31 30 29 28 27 26 25   1 2 3 4 5 6 7

ISBN 978-0-8028-8422-0

Library of Congress Cataloging-in-Publication Data

A catalog record for this book is available from the Library
of Congress.

For April

All the words

"I suppose it's only natural to think about those old boxes of sermons upstairs. They are a record of my life, after all."

—Marilynne Robinson, *Gilead*

"Someday, when you're ready, you might write our family story. Only then will you understand what happened and why."

—Norman Maclean
A River Runs through It (film)

"You write it all, discovering it at the end of the line of words."

—Annie Dillard, *The Writing Life*

Contents

Introduction: Line   *1*

PART ONE: PREPARATION

1.   Text   *11*

2.   Time   *19*

3.   Setting   *25*

4.   Prayer   *33*

PART TWO: WRITING

5.   Hook   *43*

6.   Exegesis   *49*

7.   Story   *59*

8.   Theology   *69*

9.   Thesis   *76*

10.   Resolution   *78*

PART THREE: REVISION

11.   Perspective   *85*

12.   Tension   *92*

13.   Audience   *99*

14.   Style   *105*

15.   Cuts   *115*

16.   Arrangement   *120*

17.   Critique   *123*

18.   Punctuation   *128*

Epilogue:
Final Draft   *129*

Postscript   *135*

INTRODUCTION

Line

The other day, while watching my four-year-old son, Witt, climb a magnolia tree in our front yard, I had occasion to reflect on something I had not thought about in close to forty years. I suddenly remembered how, when I was Witt's age, my own father would sometimes put me on the back of his bicycle and take me to various parks around our hometown. One park, a playground at a local Quaker church, was my favorite because of all the climbable trees that surrounded the property. I would climb, and my father would stand at the base of the tree, and I'd periodically look down to make sure he was there to catch me if I should fall.

As I stood watching Witt move from branch to branch the other day, the memory of those days came back to me—and not because of the symmetry between these moments but because of something Witt suddenly said to me.

"Do you see me, Dad?" Witt called down to me.

And I responded, "Yeah, buddy—you're *doing* it!"

To which Witt replied: "You sound like Papa when you say that."

"I do?" I asked, surprised.

INTRODUCTION

"Yeah," Witt said, nodding his head. "That's how Papa says it."

FREDERICK BUECHNER ONCE WROTE that in the final analysis, all theology is autobiographical. Having spent the past year rereading a decade's worth of my own sermons in preparation for this book, I have come to believe that Buechner was right. Because while so much has changed and improved and tightened in my preaching, one thing has remained the same: the distinctive influence others have had on my words. By this, I mean the distinctive influence of those who, for good and ill, have formed me.

Family, teachers, friends.

Those I've loved and lost.

Writers I've read and admired.

Preachers I've envied and imitated.

The list goes on.

In fact, what is most evident to me as I look back at these old sermons is that I have not only been unwittingly preaching *to* these people all this time, but they have all the while been preaching through *me*. It is stunning to revisit an old sermon and suddenly hear—in a way I was deaf to while writing it—the unmistakable accent of others.

IN 2003 I WROTE an autobiographical novel called *Storm of Fireflies*, which landed me my first literary agent. By 2007, my agent and I had revised the novel nine times, yet still the book had not been published. Finally, I gave up on it in 2008.

Storm of Fireflies then went on to sit untouched in a shoebox in my attic, where I had forgotten about it until

Line

I came across it earlier this year while searching through some files. Surprised by the nostalgia I felt upon seeing that old, familiar title, I brought the manuscript down to my living room and spent the rest of the afternoon reading it, whereupon the following line—which I don't remember writing—stole my breath:

> I ran because I was scared—scared of how broken my
> family had become and scared more by my inability
> to fix things.

Twenty years later, I can see in *Storm of Fireflies* how my voice was at the time taking shape, just as I can now see why the novel never truly landed. Most important, I can see all these years later why the novel—and its many, many drafts—were necessary for me to write. Sometimes, I now understand, we have to say a lot before we are finally ready to say anything at all. And sometimes, I now understand, we have to say a lot in order to discover a single, abiding truth.

ONE OF THE JOYFUL DISCOVERIES I made early in my tenure as a preacher is that, through its weekly rhythms and obligations, preaching is a vocation uniquely suited for self-discovery. This is something I don't think the vocational literature does a sufficient job of promoting. It certainly caught me unaware.

What I mean is that the demand of writing a weekly sermon gives the preacher a mandate to collect his or her thoughts every week and put them down in a succinct, coherent fashion. This is a remarkably clarifying require-

INTRODUCTION

ment, for the average person goes through life taking in an enormous amount of information and experiencing an infinite number of discordant things, and never has cause to try to make sense of it all. The work of coherence and concision demanded by sermon writing is therefore a built-in answer to this distinctly human dilemma.

Each week, a preacher must sift through so many ideas, and so much information, and then try to pare everything down and piece it into something not only coherent but true to what the preacher most deeply believes. Most times, it is only after the paring and piecing are done that the preacher even finds out what he or she most deeply believes. This is the unique gift of preaching. While all writers are blessed by self-discovery, preachers are the most blessed writers of all—for we have a deadline for self-discovery each Sunday.

I AM OFTEN ASKED WHERE I learned to preach, and though I later went on to study homiletics under some wonderful preacher-professors, the truth is that I originally learned how to preach through writing personal essays.

Around the time I was writing and rewriting *Storm of Fireflies*, I fell in love with Annie Dillard and Anne Lamott. Then, no sooner had I been taken with Lamott's and Dillard's creative and irreverent approach to faith and spirituality than I stumbled upon essayist Chuck Klosterman, whose then-popular book *Sex, Drugs, and Cocoa Puffs* revealed to me how irony and pop culture can be used to explore deeper, far more serious thoughts. I was in the middle of twin breakdowns at the time—faith and family—and I began writing personal essays to help myself make sense of things.

Line

Today, I doubt anyone would describe my writing or preaching as "irreverent"—and I seldom include references to pop culture in my sermons anymore—but all these years later, the style and shape I developed as an essayist through various literary influences remain as central to my sermon writing as the formal lessons I learned from various homiletical luminaries and theological giants.

THE THING ABOUT WRITING is that if you do it right and well, a great many of the words you write will prove to be unnecessary. Not unnecessary in the sense that they are inconsequential to the process but unnecessary in that they don't finally serve the point you are trying to make. This works on two levels: first, there are the words that get cut via the various rounds of edits and revisions you make; and second, there are the words that *do* make it into the final product but that—when reread years later—you realize were merely the support structure for the truly vital words. This, too, is part of the self-discovery process: you can't know what is vital, and what is merely support, and what is bound for the waste basket, until you've put in the work.

Most times, not until long after.

THERE IS A SCENE in Norman Maclean's *A River Runs through It* in which Maclean, having returned to his native Montana after four years away at Dartmouth, joins his brother, Paul, for a day of fly-fishing on the Big Blackfoot River. This was their "family river," the river on which their father had taught them how to cast a line as boys. Maclean watches Paul gracefully cast his line back and forth over the still water—performing what Paul calls "shadow cast-

INTRODUCTION

ing"—and observes that Paul, though still influenced by the form their father had taught them, has now broken free of their father's instruction and transformed his cast into a form all his own.

"I realized that in the time I was away," Maclean writes, "my brother had become an artist."

Maclean here harkens back to the book's first page, where he writes of the boys' fly-fishing lessons that, to their father, "all good things come by grace and grace comes by art and art does not come easy."

Paul had faithfully shown up to the river over and over again, each time building upon the fundamentals he'd been taught. From there, a style of his own eventually developed—an art that was distinctly his.

AS A PREACHER WHO LEARNED to write sermons by first learning to write novels and essays, this book is my attempt to explain how I go about the sermon-writing process—the method by which I've learned to cast my homiletical line. Whether the craft I have developed over the years is artful or not is for the reader to say, but I can aver that whatever is commendable in it has taken shape through showing up over and over again; by writing and rewriting; by deleting and revising—the majority of the words I've written never being seen or heard by anyone but me. Meanwhile, I can aver that my words are never my words alone, that they are indelibly marked by those I've loved and admired most—those who've raised me, taught me, hurt me, saved me. Like Witt hearing my father's voice in the inflections of my own, so too do the voices of others lurk underneath every word I've ever written; they stand at the base of every homiletical tree I've ever climbed.

Line

In that way, this book holds in tension two paradoxical truths.

First, that Count Zinzendorf is right—that we should preach the gospel, die, and be forgotten.

And second, that Miroslav Volf is also right—that nothing will be forgotten by the divine memory, and that whatever in our words is true, like whatever in our lives is true, will be raised up on the final day.

What I have learned this past year through rereading my old sermons is that the writing process itself is necessary, even though we seldom know why at the time.

"The work will become visible," Saint Paul writes to the Corinthians, "for the day will disclose it."

So too, I believe, will the *words* become visible—which is to say, if we just keep writing, the true significance of our words will one day be revealed. When all the wood, hay, and stubble of our preaching has finally been purged, it will become clear what we were trying to say, and why we were trying to say it, and who inspired us to say it, and why.

This book, then, is as much eschatological as it is homiletical, and as much autobiographical as it is methodological. I know of no other way to write it, for the art of sermon writing is as much about faith as it is about form, and more even than that, it is about faith in our words being one day transformed.

JUST YESTERDAY MY DAD SENT me a text message, and all it said was, "Love and miss you, Son."

I was dropping Witt off at preschool when the text came through, and, after reading it, I slipped my phone back in my pocket, kneeled down and zipped Witt's windbreaker

INTRODUCTION

tight, pulled him into me for a hug, and then held him slightly longer than normal. After that, I kissed him on his forehead and sent him on his way.

Some of our words—our best words—we get back.

We think they're lost; we think they've disappeared in the trash or been lost in the attic or evaporated in the air, but then, by an act of divine grace, when we least expect them, they come back again in transfigured form.

Therefore, we write by faith and not by sight—shadow casting, as it were—and we wait for the arrival of grace.

And grace comes by art, and art does not come easy.

So, for all self-discoverers aspiring to cast a line, here is everything I know about the art of writing and living a sermon.

PART ONE

PREPARATION

1

Text

I met my wife, April, two decades ago through the introduction of mutual friends, and I was smitten with her immediately. In fact, I distinctly remember that, when I first saw her, I thought that I somehow knew her, as if we'd met somewhere in a dream. Turns out I had never met her, had never even seen her, and to this day I don't know how to explain this initial sense of familiarity. My theology rules out belief in past lives and Platonic souls, so who is to say? I only mention it in order to note that, from the beginning, I felt gravitationally drawn to her.

We went on our first date not long after, and then we spent the next three years virtually inseparable. As time went on, and as it became increasingly necessary that we determine whether we would commit ourselves to "forever," I found myself growing increasingly anxious. I had no interest in dating anyone else. In fact, by this point I couldn't even imagine dating anyone else. But the fear of choice—the fear of closing the book *on* choice—terrified me.

IN *THE WRITING LIFE*, ANNIE DILLARD talks about the difficulty of first drafts and of getting our initial words

PART ONE: PREPARATION

on paper. Dillard is right about this, but for the preacher, certain difficulties must be attended to before even *getting* to that of putting pen to paper. Chief among these is the question: What will I preach *on*?

By this I don't mean *what will be my main idea*—we'll come to that—but, first, *what text will I be using*? And *why*?

It wasn't until seminary that I first heard about the Revised Common Lectionary (so low church was my upbringing), but, once discovering that such a thing existed, I have been pretty well committed to it. There are good arguments both in favor of following the lectionary and against it, and I don't intend to rehash those arguments here; I linger only long enough to say that, for me, the lectionary is my surest guard against eisegesis. When bound by a finite number of texts to choose from, I am far more likely to preach what the Spirit would have me to preach than what I, myself, might *like* to preach. For that reason, I hew pretty closely to the lectionary. That said, everything I am about to say is equally pertinent to any text we choose, whether it's from a prescribed list of suggested passages or from the entire biblical corpus.

So—we begin by reading the passages. By prayerfully reading them. By soliciting the help of the Spirit in indicating what text *wants* to be preached. If, like me, you're following the lectionary, you'll have four passages to read. If not, you'll be trusting the Spirit to guide you to (and through) any number of possible passages.

This part of the process is not to be rushed.

In our eagerness to get to the actual writing, we can easily become like Paul and his companions setting sail for Bithynia when the Holy Spirit has plans for us in Philippi.

Text

Which is to say, just because a passage may be interesting to us or may seem particularly sermon-worthy does not mean it's the passage the Spirit is drawing us toward. I have many times, on account of poor discernment, preached a Bithynian sermon and, in consequence, spent a long Sunday afternoon ruing my failure to preach toward Philippi.

We read, therefore, carefully. All the while asking ourselves:

- What is the passage trying to say?
- What do we remember—before even consulting our commentaries—about the particular book the passage comes from?
- What energy do we feel moving us—and moving *in* us—as we read?
- How might this passage be pertinent to what's happening *now*—both in the wider world and, even more importantly, in our particular congregation?

The answers to these questions may not at first be obvious, but, eventually, if we don't rush it, the answers will begin to present themselves. And when they do, and when the answers begin to point toward a single text in particular, we do well to make the choice, commit to it, and not look back.

I HAVE ONLY HAD THREE recurring dreams in my life. In the first, I am about to get married, and I am at a wedding venue, and I am dressed for the occasion, and I am riddled with anxiety. Details in the dream are always hazy, and who I am marrying is always beside the point, for the dream never gets that far. Instead, the dream always ends abruptly.

PART ONE: PREPARATION

Suddenly, my father appears.

And I tell him that I am scared—that I don't know whether I should go through with it.

And my father says to me: "Don't do it."

And I run away.

WE CAN'T GO ON DELIBERATING forever on what text we'll preach. If we do, we'll never preach anything at all. Therefore, we must commit to the text we've chosen—that is, we share it with our music minister and our children's minister and our office manager and whoever else might be dependent on or affected by our choice—and we don't look back. Then, from the moment we have selected it, we keep covenant with it; and not because of a dogged stubbornness but because of a sincere trust—no, better: because of a faithful *conviction*—that this is the text the Holy Spirit has drawn us to.

IT'S HARD TO OVERSTATE HOW wonderful my childhood was. How loved and provided for I was by both of my parents. How close my family always was. How protected and safe I always felt.

It came as a great surprise to me, then, when around the age of fifteen my dad started telling me to be leery of marriage.

"You're a good-looking kid, Austin," he began to say to me. "And girls are drawn to you. Which is great. But just remember that you have a long life ahead of you. And you don't want to be tied down."

I remember looking back at him blankly, an uneasy feel-

Text

ing coming over me, because even at fifteen I could infer the subtext of what he was saying.

"Don't get me wrong," he continued. "I love your mother. But if I had it to do over again, I would never have gotten married so young."

Again: blank stare.

"I just don't want you to make a mistake," he finished, sensing that I was uncomfortable. "All I'm saying is, keep your options open. And enjoy your life. Because responsibilities start building up right away—and when they do, they are like chains."

ONCE WE HAVE COMMITTED TO a text, the work of clarifying our sermon's thesis begins. What will we *do* with this text that we've chosen? It is one thing to commit to a text; it is an entirely other thing to commit to a direction for preaching it. Therefore, with our text chosen, we do well to resume the important work of prayerful reading.

Personally, I tend to reread the passage in question at least ten times, each time listening carefully for a summons from the Spirit. Somehow, this summons always comes. And when it does, it works like magnetism, like gravity slowly pulling me toward a specific verse. And then a specific phrase *in* that verse.

An example: On Epiphany Sunday, my text was Matthew 2:1–12. As I read and reread the text, I remembered past sermons I'd preached from the passage, fondly recalling the way that "by another route" had once been the phrase that had summoned me, and how it had been "he was disturbed" a different time. Some of these sermons—preached years and years ago—came back to me with a

PART ONE: PREPARATION

fuzzy familiarity. This time, though, read and reread as I might, no gravitational pull was yet occurring.

Until, suddenly, it was.

On about my seventh reading of the passage, verse 11 began to draw my attention. And, as it did, I narrowed my focus to attend to what it might be trying to reveal to me.

> On coming to the house, they saw the child with his mother Mary, and they bowed down and worshiped him. (NIV)

I lingered over the sentence.

I asked myself: Does what's drawing me to this sentence have to do with the magi's experience of "coming to the house"? Is it about the *kind* of house—its humble nature?

This, I felt, wasn't it. At least, it wasn't the center of what I was being pulled toward.

So, I continued to ask more questions: Is it about the significance of the magi bowing down? Is it about what genuflection says about the holiness they were encountering? Or is it perhaps about the magi's reflexive act of worship?

I knew in my spirit that none of these were quite it, either.

And then, just like that, a phrase pulled me even closer: "They saw the child."

With this, it all suddenly began to register, the gravity now pulling me to solid ground. It was to be a sermon about the way the rest of the world was looking right past this humble child, assuming—as we are all prone to assuming—that divine revelation would only appear in places we expect to see it, while the magi, these "foreigners from afar," looked with a more refined sense of perception and *saw* him.

Just like that, I now had not only a text to preach from

Text

but an anchor *in* the text out of which to chart my sermon's course.

THE FREEDOM TO CHOOSE IS a double-edged sword: anything is possible, but this means that *anything* is possible. So, given the innumerable choices that human beings face, and taking into account the immensity of a lifetime, how do we know we're choosing rightly? How do we know that, once we've started down one path, we won't be best advised to turn around and seek out another? And then another after that? What's the criteria by which we choose how to act; how to begin; how to move forward; how to live?

I raise such existential questions because, though on a far less weighty scale, these are the same questions that haunt the preacher as he or she tries to decide what to preach each Sunday. That is why, in both sermon writing and life, it is important to have a rationale for paring things down and knowing where to begin. Eventually, we have to make a decision and commit to it, because to spend all week selecting a text is to render preaching impossible, just as leaving our options open indefinitely is to forestall living a full human life.

THAT SAID, MISTAKES CAN BE made. We *can* choose wrongly. We *can* find ourselves stuck in a Bithynian sermon or, worse, in a Bithynian marriage. So, what's to save us from a life of ambivalence?

In my experience, it's the Spirit of God working in the same way it worked on Day One. Which is to say, the Spirit hovers over all that is formless and void in our lives, over all the infinite possibilities that, both homiletically and existentially, abide at first as mere potentialities.

PART ONE: PREPARATION

As it hovers, the Spirit whispers directives that, if we will open ourselves to its voice and follow its lead, will bring order and structure and purpose and beauty into the uncertainty that otherwise overwhelms us. Each time we listen to the Spirit, each time we surrender to its quiet pull, the stronger its next whisper will be, its force amassing like gravity—step by step, choice by choice, word by word, line by line—pulling us closer and closer to the holy end to which it is calling us.

2

Time

The thing April and I most frequently fought about in our early years of marriage was money. Not just because of how little we had of it, but because of how irresponsible I was with what we had. It wasn't that I was a spendthrift; it's that I simply paid no attention to our monthly budget. For April, certain items took priority over others, and each bill was due at a certain time each month, and there was a finite figure that circumscribed how we could live within these financial realities. For me, however, the month was like a lazy river, something I floated along each month with staggering nonchalance, oblivious to where we were in the monthly flow of things. I was like Wilkins Micawber in *David Copperfield*, ever-optimistic that "something will turn up" to solve our desperate financial situation and willfully reluctant to check our bank account lest our balance dampen my optimism.

I distinctly remember April crying one afternoon because of how trapped she felt—trapped in a job she resented, in an old house she didn't like and couldn't afford to

PART ONE: PREPARATION

fix up, in a marriage that (though she didn't say so) would not bend in line with its financial realities.

"What would you *like* to do?" I asked her, my earnestness no doubt grating. "What's your dream?"

She just stared at me.

"Seriously," I said. "Whatever it is, you can do it. *We* can do it. We can make it happen. If you just tell me what it is, we'll do it."

With tears in her eyes, tears born more of exasperation and exhaustion than of anger and anxiety, she replied: "Can't you see what I'm trying to tell you? I'm telling you we're not going to *make* it, and you respond by turning into Jim Valvano!"

EACH WEEK FOR A PREACHER is like a river, like an ever-flowing stream, and it comes at us fast. No sooner have we delivered last Sunday's sermon than the following Sunday is upon us, and it is up to us to know how best to budget our time to ensure that we are indeed ready. When do we do the prayerful reading and the text selection we discussed in the last chapter? When do we begin to consult our commentaries and our other homiletical resources? When do we actually sit down to write? When do we do the various rounds of revisions that will inevitably be necessary?

In a seven-day stretch wherein sermon writing is but one of our vocational responsibilities—no greater of a priority than hospital visits, pastoral care, funerals, weddings, staff meetings, committee meetings, civic responsibilities, and general church oversight—we must be aware of where we are in the river's flow, or else we will soon enough find ourselves sinking in it.

Time

MY GRANDFATHER, MY MOM'S DAD, was the first radiologist in my hometown, a 1936 Duke Med grad who carved out a respectable name and a nice living for my mom's family. When he passed away in 1991, what my parents received from his estate was quite generous. On top of that, my dad was a successful salesman, his charm and sincerity a powerful professional combination. It didn't hurt that he looked like Kevin Costner.

Consequently, I grew up very comfortable, never wanting for anything. All the while, I moved through life blissfully oblivious to my family's social and financial reality—blissfully oblivious, that is, to what was making such easy living possible—and it seemed a matter of course to me that things would always go this way.

As I came of age, I don't recall having any conversations with my parents about money—about how to earn it, how to use it, how to save it, how to conceptualize it. I do, however, remember how my parents encouraged me to pursue my dreams, to do whatever I felt called to do, just as I remember how entirely sincere and unconditional their encouragement always was.

IF EACH WEEK FOR A preacher is indeed a river, I spent the first year of my ministry drowning in it. Some weeks I'd spend as much as three days reading commentaries and making notes and mentally preparing myself for the sermon-writing task. Other weeks, I'd find myself inundated with hospital visits and other such duties and scrambling even to *get* to my sermon writing. Looking back a decade later, I see now a young man paddling hard upriver, the currents coming at him faster and faster, and I get exhausted even thinking about it.

PART ONE: PREPARATION

What saved me was the counsel of a mentor, a seasoned preacher who said to me: "Austin, you have to budget your week the way you budget your finances."

Not really having a budget *for* my finances, not really knowing how such a thing even worked, I simply looked at him and waited for him to continue.

"It's not like you spend money out of your food allocation on clothing," he said, "and it's not like you spend money out of your mortgage allocation on gas, so don't spend your sermon time on administration and don't spend your prep time on pastoral care. *Balance* these things."

Nonplussed, I responded, "How does that work?"

"Easy," he told me. "You just set aside a few specific hours early in your week for sermon prep, and then you set aside a specific day each week for sermon writing. And then—and this is the crucial part—then you treat that day as sacrosanct."

"That's what *you* do?" I asked him.

He nodded. "If I don't, I'll spend each day going back and forth to my computer, tinkering with the sermon and then putting it aside, and I'll neglect other important responsibilities while doing it. That, or I won't even *touch* the sermon, and then Saturday night will arrive and I'll have nothing to preach the next morning."

"That's exactly how my weeks feel right now," I confided in him.

"I know," he replied. "Which is why I am saying: *budget*."

AROUND THIS SAME TIME, I HAPPENED to be reading George Eliot's *Middlemarch*, and I found myself struck by Eliot's description of Tertius Lydgate, the capable and sin-

Time

cere town doctor whose laissez-faire approach to money was, by this point in the novel, becoming a burden on his marriage and career.

> He had a reverential soul with a strong practical intelligence. But he could not manage finance; he knew values well, but he had no keenness of imagination for monetary results in the shape of profit and loss.

April and I now had two young children, daughters just beginning preschool, and our monthly obligations were growing. Yet still I had not overcome my nonchalance about such things, my "unconquerable indifference to money" as Eliot writes of Tertius Lydgate. As I read these words, the scales began to fall from my eyes, because I saw myself in Lydgate and did not like what I was looking at.

That night, once the girls were asleep, I approached April and apologized to her for years of obtuseness. Apologized not only for my unhelpfulness in balancing our monthly budget but for my childish optimism regarding how, despite our meager budget, we could make all our dreams and desires come true. I vowed that night to try to become more of a realist, someone more attuned to what is possible and what is not; someone more aware of the difference between healthy hope and misguided optimism.

Beginning that night, we began to budget, opening separate bank accounts for recurring bills, groceries, restaurants, gas, clothing, savings, and miscellany. Slowly, I came to see the beauty of a balanced budget, of the way that knowing *what* is being allocated *where*—of knowing where we are in the river—brings with it a deep sense of peace.

PART ONE: PREPARATION

THIS IS ALL A LONG way of saying: carve out a day of your week and make *that* your sermon-writing day. I'll say more later about sermon prep and about edits and revisions, but for now I simply leave you with this: budget your week the way you budget your bank account, making sermon writing the part of your budget that takes up the most space and receives the most advance priority in budgetary preparation. I personally write on Thursdays, and over time this has become an anchor for me in the week, a tree I can cling to in the rushing river of pastoral responsibilities. That said, whether your day be Thursday or Monday—or Tuesday or Friday or *any* day—simply *pick* a day and commit to it.

IT'S HARD ALL THESE YEARS later to think about the night my dad told my mother that our family would be declaring bankruptcy, that his business was down and that we were deeply in debt and that there was no other way around it.

I wasn't there for this conversation, of course—it was all my dad could do to speak of it to my mom, let alone share such things with my sister and me—so I only learned of it after the news had been delivered, after my dad had driven away in shame and sorrow and regret.

I remember holding my mom as she cried that night, telling her that we were okay, that all was going to be okay, that all would work out just fine.

I believed all of this. I really did. Such childlike optimism was all I knew how to offer then. This kind of earnest positivity was the gift my parents had given me, and now it was becoming the burden that I'd have to bear.

3

Setting

A year or so ago I was standing in our kitchen, hidden behind our pantry door, shoveling Oreos into my mouth as quickly as I could. My hiddenness was not accidental; I'd purposely kept the pantry door open to keep my family from seeing what I was doing. Around this time, certain pressures at my church were bringing me a great deal of anxiety. Meanwhile, our home needed numerous repairs that we couldn't afford to fix; our youngest son, Bennett, was barely a year old and was rarely sleeping through the night; we had four children under the age of eight who rightly needed (and demanded) our attention; and I'd recently gotten a call from my sister that had thrown me right back into the vortex of a family drama I'd been running from for over a decade. Generally speaking, I was in a bad place.

So, I turned to the Oreos.

Standing there that afternoon, thinking I was safely protected by the open pantry door, I suddenly heard Witt at my feet; he'd approached me so quietly that I had not even registered him coming around the opposite corner.

PART ONE: PREPARATION

"Why do you do that?" he asked.

"Do what?" I responded.

"Close your eyes and eat like that?"

Surprised, defensive, I said: "I don't."

Witt nodded. "Yes, you do. You come over here and you eat cookies and you close your eyes like that when you eat them."

BEYOND SELECTING A SPECIFIC DAY for sermon writing, it is necessary to cultivate a liturgical approach *to* the day. By which I mean a routine to follow: a disciplined plan for where we will write, what time we will begin, what we will surround ourselves with, what coffee mug we will drink from, where we will put our cell phones, and any number of related, seemingly mundane issues.

Early in my ministry I thought that items such as these were unimportant, things that could be negotiated from week to week, things that I could just "feel my way through" as I went. Thus, I'd write some days in my office and other days at coffee shops; some days I'd write from home and other days from hidden rooms in the back of my church. I'd begin some mornings at nine and other mornings as late as eleven; some days I'd schedule meetings through lunch and not even open my computer until two in the afternoon.

And, for a while, this was fine.

But then, soon enough, I began to notice that things were feeling increasingly out of control. And, with this lack of control came an abiding sense of anxiety and dis-ease— a sense of somehow being trapped by the immensity of it all. (Let us not forget: writing a sermon is *hard*.) Thus, I'd finally sit down to write and then a pastoral care call would

Setting

come in and I would have to sprint back out; or I'd get started on the sermon only to get helplessly distracted by things happening out my office window; or I'd be midway through a first draft and it would suddenly be time for me to pick up my kids from preschool—and on and on. Fortunately, around this time I came across a counterintuitive line from Richard Foster's *Celebration of Discipline*.

"Discipline brings freedom."

As I reflected on these words, I found myself thinking about a great many things in my life—from my approach to food and finances to my approach to significant relationships and daily leisure—and I felt convicted by the liberality with which I approached such things and by how this liberality issued not in a greater sense of freedom but in an increasingly anxious form of exhaustion.

Beginning that day, I tried to tighten certain areas of my life, areas ranging from my diet to my closest relationships, and among those areas was my approach to sermon writing and the conditions that surround and support it.

ONE OF MY EARLIEST MEMORIES is of being at home in the afternoons with my mom, the sky beginning to darken, and my dad calling from work and asking my mom to put a beer in the freezer because he was about to head home. Back in those days he would seldom have more than one beer. Instead, he'd come home, he'd greet my mother, he'd pick me up and ask me how my day had been, and then he'd take me outside to play and he'd encourage me profusely in whatever I was playing ("You're *doing* it, buddy!). Soon we'd have dinner, and he'd drink his beer, and we'd watch television, and then he and my mom would put me in bed,

PART ONE: PREPARATION

where they'd pray with me before leaving the room. Then, back in his room, he'd read his Bible each night while my mom would read magazines or watch television, and then they would turn out their light and go to sleep.

For years, until I was about fifteen, that Bible would sit by his bedside each night.

IF DISCIPLINE BRINGS FREEDOM, IT also brings creativity. I was amazed by how a more disciplined approach to the conditions of my sermon-writing process—by attending to the arrangement of the homiletical furniture that surrounded me—led to greater imagination and clarity of thought. In those early days, I'd begin at 10:00 a.m. sharp and I'd write in coffee shops. Over time, though, I found that a quieter environment was necessary. I tried to write from home; but with young children in and out of day care and with April often working from home, that didn't work. So, finally, I committed myself to writing from my office, but I made it clear to our office staff and to my ministerial colleagues that, unless there was a pressing matter, I was "out of office" on Thursdays until the writing process was finished. Around this same time, I committed to a slightly earlier start time—9:00 a.m.—because my kids' morning routines had by this point become slightly more manageable.

Today, this remains my "where" and my "when." Other parts of my weekly discipline include closing my blinds (Annie Dillard says we can never be too guarded against distractions); having my preferred coffee mug in hand (a wide-rimmed mug from my favorite bookstore); having

Setting

my preferred NRSV Bible to the left of my laptop (sitting on an otherwise empty desk); and having any commentaries or books I plan to use stacked on a desk just behind me.

From there, I put my phone on silent and place it in the top drawer of my desk; I sit quietly and reflect for a few minutes on the thesis to which the Spirit's gravity has pulled me and to which I've already committed; I open a new Word document and behold anew the weekly burden of a blank page; and then—I pray.

IT WASN'T HARD TO NOTICE when my dad's drinking became a problem. Even though it would take me years—well over a decade—to acknowledge it *as* a problem, the sheer obviousness of it, not to mention the demonstrable effects it was having on our family, was clear from the very beginning. His one daily beer quickly became a great many daily beers, and whereas he'd once stayed close to home each evening with our family, he soon began running certain nights with a rowdy, lewd bunch. I, myself, was in high school at the time, drinking as much and as often as I possibly could—running with a crew far rowdier and far lewder than the one my dad was running with—so I didn't think too much of it. In fact, what little I *did* think of it I thought was pretty cool.

Soon enough, he and I started drinking together, my dad buying beer for me and my friends and then, later, my dad coming with us to the bars, hanging with us until the wee hours of the morning.

When I finally began to realize what a problem it had become; when I finally began to sense—though not yet in

PART ONE: PREPARATION

an articulable way—that I was angry about it, furious even, and that I resented what it was doing to him, to our lives, to our family—around this time I saw him one day pulling into our driveway, getting out of his car, and hiding his empty beer cans in the bushes. I had quietly watched him do this exact thing any number of times by this point, but this time—who's to say why—I went out and approached him about it.

"Why do you do that?" I asked.

"Do what?" he said, clearly surprised and defensive.

"Throw your empty beer cans in the bushes."

"I don't," he said.

"Yes, you do," I said. "You come over here and you throw your cans in the bushes and then you come in the house as if you haven't been drinking at all."

IN *CELEBRATION OF DISCIPLINE* FOSTER powerfully distinguishes between discipline and addiction, between good habits and bad. And the thing that stuck with me through the years is how right Foster is—how discipline *does* bring about freedom.

We might think it's a function of freedom to write when we want; and where we want; and how we want. We might think it's unnecessarily restrictive and burdensome to adopt a specific process for such things and to abide by that process with utter faithfulness. Just as we might think it is unnecessarily burdensome to limit ourselves to one or two drinks a day, or to one or two desserts a week, or to one or two hours of television each night, or—to up the ante even further—to a lifetime commitment to one person, or

Setting

to one vocation, or to one hometown, or to one home *in* that town. The scale of such things varies, but the principle is the same: what seems like true freedom often leads to feelings of abiding despair, and what seem like oppressive constraints often lead to feelings of true freedom.

So, in the same way that we do well to cultivate good habits and spiritual disciplines in our lives, and in the same way that what at first seems manageable without such discipline has a way of sliding out of control before we even recognize it, so too is it with the discipline and habit of sermon writing. Which is why we do well to pick a day; pick a time; pick a place; secure the conditions; and abide by these constraints with disciplined faithfulness. If we do that, the seemingly trivial nature of these commitments will issue in a clarity and creativity that will astonish us.

THAT SAID, THE APOSTLE PAUL contends that the spirit is willing but the flesh is weak—and he is right. For even after committing ourselves to certain constraints, and trying faithfully and fervently to live *by* them, burdens and pressures and stresses and shames can waylay us at any moment. On one level, this means we can be months or even years into a faithful discipline of weekly sermon writing and then, suddenly, the demands of the job or the complexities of life can throw us spinning back into the chaotic routines from which we've come. In the same way but on a far deeper level, commitments to healthier eating and to healthier living can be jettisoned in a stressful second, just as relapses happen to hundreds of addicts every single day.

PART ONE: PREPARATION

It happens.

Nothing is a sure safeguard.

This I've learned the hard way.

But the desire to tame it, the belief in the power of the constraint, is the thing we absolutely must cultivate as preachers.

ANOTHER TEXT, THIS ONE at night. Too late at night.

Hey Son! Blues Traveler! 90s were the best!

An old familiar ache surfaces as I put the phone back on my side table, resting it atop the Bible that sits there each night.

4

Prayer

When my grandmother died a few years ago at the age of ninety-eight, April and I sat the kids down and gently broke the news to them. While our older children, our daughters Ada and Julianna, were aware of elderly church members who had passed in their lifetime, this was the first family member they'd ever lost. To be expected, they were sad and confused.

So where *is* Great-ama, they wanted to know? And why did she have to die?

April and I did our best to assure the girls of Great-ama's love for them; of how she is now being held in God's eternal care and of how natural it is for them to feel sad about it. We then took turns sharing special memories of our time with her, each girl remembering things my grandmother said to them or did with them.

And that was that.

The discussion ended, and the tears dried, and we went back to our daily lives.

Days later, though, as I was tucking the girls into bed, Julianna suddenly said, "Can we pray for Great-ama tonight?"

PART ONE: PREPARATION

To which Ada responded, "How can we pray for Great-ama, JuJu? She's dead."

Julianna looked to me. "Can we not pray for dead people, Daddy?"

I didn't answer.

"Daddy?" Ada asked, as if prompting me to speak.

"Well," I finally said. "Many Christians pray for the dead."

Ada looked at me funny. "How do you do *that*?" she asked. "How do you even know what to say?"

WITH OUR TEXT SELECTED AND our writing day picked and our process defined and our constraints in place, we have one thing left to do as preachers before we face the blank page: pray.

To me, this is the most nonnegotiable part of the sermon-writing process, and not because it's the most overtly spiritual aspect but because it is the most centering, preparatory, mysterious, and life-giving part.

Just think: here before us is that familiar blinking cursor, that overwhelming blank page, and, somehow, we know we must fill it once more with the proper words. Whence comes the energy? The inspiration? The clarity?

The substance—not to mention the spirit—of what we write will inevitably be diminished if we think it is entirely up to us to pull off this Herculean feat. Thus, a centering and supplicatory prayer is vital.

But then comes the question: What is it in such a moment that we are praying *for*?

MY GRANDMOTHER, MY DAD'S MOM, was a remarkable woman. Raised on an Iowa farm, one of six children, she

34

Prayer

excelled in school and ultimately graduated summa cum laude from college with a triple major. She was offered a full scholarship to study philosophy at the University of Chicago but turned it down to marry my grandfather. Years later, while living in Germany during World War II and raising five boys, she took it upon herself to learn Russian, becoming so proficient in the language that she was later contracted by the National Academy of Sciences to translate a major work on geology from Russian to English.

Her intellect being what it was, she had little time for religion. She identified as Christian and dutifully attended church, but her participation was more civic than it was pious; more social than it was religious.

This all changed, though, when she was forty-five. Suddenly, Christian faith became *everything* to her: the very lens through which she interpreted reality.

For years I would ask her about this sudden conversion, this transition from casual commitment to robust belief, and always she said she had been "overcome by the Holy Spirit." Unsatisfied, I would press her to elaborate, and she tried her best to provide a more sufficient response, but always she came back to this mysterious answer. Ever the philosopher, she explained that because language is a human construct, it is therefore limited. "Which means," she said, "there are some things that words simply cannot capture." This always felt like a cop-out to me, because I believed that if you couldn't explain something or make sense of something, then it was likely because it was complete nonsense.

But I loved my grandmother, so I would humor her and press no further.

PART ONE: PREPARATION

One day, though, I was home from college and chatting with her about a course I was taking on the philosophy of language, and she stunned me by connecting Ludwig Wittgenstein's *Tractatus* to the apostle Paul's letter to the Romans.

"When our 'language games' fail," she said to me, "God's Spirit intercedes for us with sighs too deep for words."

Impressed by her ability to quote both of these writers from memory, I said, "That's amazing, Grandma. But what does that *mean*?"

"We don't know," she responded. "And that's the point."

I didn't agree with her, but I didn't know what else to say. We therefore sat in silence for several seconds.

Finally, my grandmother said, "Here's the best I can explain it. Most times when I pray for you, I pray for specific things. I pray that you'll be kept safe from harm; that you'll do well in school; that you'll be loving and generous with others. Things like that. But *sometimes*"—and here she paused—"*sometimes* I recognize how insufficient these prayers are, how far they are from conveying my deepest hopes for you and how limited my language is to express these things; so, in those moments, I stop speaking and I sit in silence, trusting that Paul is right: that when we know not how to pray, God's Spirit will intercede for us, translating that for which we have no words into that which we most need to say."

AS PREACHERS SITTING BEFORE A blinking cursor, do we pray for creativity? For eloquence? For clarity of thought? Or do we pray for more overtly theological things? Things like words that will open hearts to the resurrected Jesus or that will convict of sin and shortcoming or that will in-

Prayer

spire kingdom-building action in the world? Do we invoke biblical language, praying that God's will might be done, or that we might be used as vessels, or that the words of our mouths and the meditations of our hearts might be pleasing unto God?

Surely, all these prayers are pertinent and appropriate and no doubt advisable. But do they get at what we are really asking for, hoping for, yearning for, *looking* for when we are about to begin writing a sermon?

I DID NOT ELABORATE that night Ada asked me how we could pray for the dead. My girls were too young for me to explain to them what the apostle Paul means by "sighs too deep for words," and if my grandmother could not convey to me as a college student what she meant by the "limitations of human language," how could I possibly convey the idea to a couple of elementary-aged children?

But weeks after my grandmother's passing, as we were back in my hometown for my grandmother's memorial and were at her house going through her things, I found myself thinking about what I told my girls that night—about how we sometimes pray our best prayers when we don't know what to say.

At the time, I was listening to family members tell stories about my grandmother's long and full life. Aunts were describing various hardships she'd undergone; an uncle talked about a late-term miscarriage; a cousin talked about the difficulty of losing three sons to cancer; my dad talked about the complications she endured as a mother of five in Germany. I heard stories about her alcoholic father and her alcoholic brother; I heard the whole family laugh as they

PART ONE: PREPARATION

remembered how religiously she'd exercised her whole life, how disciplined she was in all that she'd said and done.

As I listened to these stories, I happened to be holding a framed photograph of my grandmother as a young girl, her whole life still before her. How much she didn't yet know, I thought. How much she *couldn't* yet know. Which made me suddenly think of my own children. Of how much lies before them in their own lives, almost all of which I can't yet know how to pray for.

There is so much I hope for my children. So much I wish to protect them from and so little I truly can. So much I realize I am burdening them with without even knowing it; so little I can do to become aware of what these things are, let alone cut such things out.

Staring at this ninety-year-old photograph of my grandmother, I was suddenly overwhelmed by how small and limited I am in the scheme of things, of how small and limited we all are, and I suddenly understood what my grandmother meant when she said that her prayers for me were too often insufficient on their own. And just as suddenly, like my grandmother long before me, I too felt "overcome by the Holy Spirit."

And so, with great intentionality, I stood staring at that photograph, thinking of my children, thinking of them in the present moment and thinking of the unknown future that awaits them all, and, as I did, I somehow knew that I was praying one of the best prayers that I had ever prayed, even though I knew not what I was saying.

WE CAN'T KNOW AS PREACHERS what to pray for as we prepare ourselves to write a sermon. For, by its very nature, what we are about to attempt is an absurdity. An impossibility.

Prayer

To speak about God? To speak *for* God?

Yet somehow each of us feels—no: each of us knows—that we have nonetheless been called *by* God to this very thing. To this very moment.

And so, with fear and trembling, we do well to center ourselves and to take on a posture of supplication, and then, while staring at that blank page, to sit quietly and reverentially, trusting that our prayers are often most incisive when spoken through sighs too deep for words.

PART TWO

WRITING

5

Hook

"I hate Coldplay."

This sentiment, from the opening of Chuck Klosterman's *Sex, Drugs, and Cocoa Puffs*, has had a profound effect on my approach to sermon writing. In an essay *really* about the shallowness of modern relationships and contemporary culture, Klosterman begins his argument by sounding off on the renowned British pop band.

Reading this essay in 2004, I had never encountered such a jarring use of misdirection, and it thrilled me. So much so that I began to incorporate it in my own writing, spending years trying to use pop culture as a hook for my own essays (and, later, for my own sermons). Today, I don't tend to be as on the nose with this kind of misdirection—which I will soon begin referring to as "parallelism"—but, to this day, the power of this rhetorical technique still informs the way I typically begin a sermon. The key, of course, is to make your audience think you're talking about "this" when really, at a far deeper level, you're talking about "that."

This device is so effective because it taps into the way we most effectively learn as human beings, which is through

PART TWO: WRITING

metaphor. In *I Is an Other: The Secret Life of Metaphor and How It Shapes the Way We See the World*, James Geary explains that metaphors are the means by which we come to understand abstract ideas. "This is the primary purpose of metaphor: to carry over existing names or descriptions to things that are either so new they haven't yet been named or so abstract they cannot be otherwise explained."

Through telling a story, or through talking about something entirely other than the point we intend to make, we can help readers and listeners better apprehend our ultimate point via the joy of association. As Geary demonstrates, the brain excretes significant amounts of dopamine as it makes a connection between seemingly disparate things—through connecting how "this" is not only related to but is representative of "that"—and this neural sweetener helps us as preachers get and keep a listener's attention.

AROUND THE TIME APRIL and I got married, I began to shy away from alcohol. This sudden change surprised both of us, because up until this point I had always been more than happy to take a drink. Now, though, I was turning down all such offers and opportunities, telling friends and colleagues that I preferred to be clear-eyed and clearheaded, that I just didn't have the desire for it anymore. I assumed this was just a function of getting older and more mature, that it was something that naturally attended my commitment to marriage and to the future that April and I were building together. For years—for well over a decade—this was how I explained and understood my sudden abstemiousness.

Hook

ANOTHER REASON IT IS HELPFUL to begin a sermon with misdirection is that the thing we really intend to say, the point we really want to make, is often hard and heavy, and writing about something lighter or more playful can be a helpful way into saying it. In fact, we often learn what we want to say about the *real* point by first feeling out the contours of the metaphor we are making. In my experience, our own understanding of a point actually gets stretched and clarified by setting it alongside something different and then showing how the two things are not unlike at all.

I'VE HEARD THE INCOMPARABLE PREACHER Tom Long talk about the art of sermon design and how it is like the installation of window panels. What I take Long to mean is that, as he is about to begin, he can see in his mind's eye several different "panels" of an as-yet-empty window frame. That he has a sense of what panels ought to go in the window and of how he, as the designer, intends to arrange them.

I can think of no better image to explain this initial part of the process.

Like Long, I too "see" several sections that will help me marshal my argument, and I have a hazy vision for the order in which these sections might best be arranged. In coming chapters I will address how seldom this initial vision aligns with the final product, but for now I simply want to present the idea of a subdivided structure—the pieces of homiletical paneling.

The first piece of homiletical paneling to be considered is the opening image, the metaphor that will serve as a cipher for the larger point the sermon seeks to make.

PART TWO: WRITING

In other words, the Coldplay panel.

When Klosterman started that essay by citing his hatred for Coldplay, he didn't intend to write a piece about why he didn't like Coldplay; he intended to write an essay about why he didn't like the emotional manipulation that drives the contemporary entertainment industry. However, saying "I hate Coldplay" is a lot more effective at piquing a reader's interest than diving headlong into a treatise on the intersection of enlightenment romanticism and late-stage capitalism. Eventually, of course, it becomes clear that what Coldplay's music represents in the essay is the manufactured emotionalism that defines our distorted idea of twenty-first-century love, but, at first, we think Klosterman simply has an axe to grind with Chris Martin because Klosterman's girlfriend once dumped him to go see a Coldplay concert.

In the same way, beginning a sermon with an image or a statement or a concept that, at first blush, has seemingly little relationship to the Scripture passage at hand rouses the congregation's interest and catalyzes their neurons.

For instance, a few weeks ago—in a sermon on Mark 1:29–39—the gravity of the Scripture had pulled me to verse 37, where the disciples say to Jesus, "Everyone is searching for you" (NRSV). My thesis was that, in saying this, the disciples were unwittingly giving voice to a universal human longing—how we are *all* searching for Jesus; how, like Augustine says, our hearts are restless until they find their rest in him. But rather than begin by quoting this famous line from Augustine (which indeed would be used in one panel), or by discussing our alienation from God (which would take place

Hook

in another panel), or by enumerating the countless places we go in search of finding God (which would take place in yet another panel), I opened with an image from the final page of Harper Lee's *To Kill a Mockingbird*.

> I willed myself to stay awake, but the rain was so soft and the room was so warm and my father's voice was so deep and his knee was so snug that I slept.

All I said in this opening panel was that I wanted everyone to picture this child in her father's lap: feeling so loved, so provided for, so watched over, so *safe*, that she soon drifts off into a peaceful rest. From there, I shifted gears into a recapitulation of verses 35–37. And, with that, the Coldplay panel was now properly placed. It wasn't until much later in the sermon that I would loop back to the Coldplay panel and demonstrate how Scout Finch's rest in her father's lap—after an experience of deep emotional overwhelm—is analogous to the rest we are all searching for, a rest that can only be found in the lap of the resurrected Christ Jesus.

This, of course, is but one example of how to do this.

We'll talk in a coming chapter about the parallelism required throughout a sermon to ensure that, once we *do* loop back to the Coldplay panel, the association is fittingly made and the connection comes as both a surprise and as a source of clarity for the listener. For now, though, we'll leave off here, with the importance of a strong opening that piques the listener's interest and that (at first) veils the larger point we want to make.

PART TWO: WRITING

IT WAS ONLY A FEW years ago that it dawned on me why I no longer like to drink alcohol. Why the idea of it turns my stomach, and why I find myself quietly resentful of friends when they become drunk in my presence. I realize how obtuse this makes me sound, but it's the truth: I somehow never made the connection between my sudden abstention and the effect my father's alcoholism had had on me and my family.

It all came to me one night in an otherwise anodyne conversation with a ministerial colleague who asked me why I wasn't drinking with the rest of the ministers gathered. I'd been asked this exact question numerous times before—hundreds, probably—but this time I suddenly heard myself say, "My dad is an alcoholic."

And there it was: a connection made—long after the initial presentation.

I assure you it was both surprising and clarifying.

6

Exegesis

Here's another thing I've heard Tom Long say: "Come summer time, everyone wants to feel the cool of an air conditioner, but no one wants to hear the HVAC rumbling right beside their ear."

I think of this advice nearly every time I begin panel number two, the exegesis panel.

Every congregation wants—or at least, every congregation *should* want—to know that their preacher has done serious research and exegetical work in preparation for the sermon; but no congregant wants to be immersed in the minutia of ancient Near East arcana or intramural scholarly debates. It should therefore be clear to congregants by what we *do* present in our sermons that we are speaking from a wealth of background information, but we must also be hip to what benefits the sermon's thesis and moves it forward and what only serves to bog it down.

WHEN I WAS TAKING clinical pastoral education (CPE) as a seminarian, I would periodically meet with my supervisor to discuss how things were going. And, in those meetings,

PART TWO: WRITING

she would press me to be more open with her about myself, about what I'd been through in my life and about why I had a tendency to redirect conversation whenever she'd try to ask about my childhood and my family.

One day, I began to tell her about an afternoon when I was about eight years old and was in the car with my mom and a certain song came on the radio. The song, I told her, was about wishing you could go back in time and be with someone you dated when you were younger, but how you can't go back again, how there's no use giving in, and how you just have to deal with it. And I told my supervisor about how my mom turned the song up as it played, and how, when it ended, she told me that the song was right, that life is difficult and that we never know whether the choices we make are the right ones.

The supervisor looked at me and waited for me to go on. When I didn't, she prompted me: "So, you sensed she was talking about herself?"

Uncomfortable, I redirected: "We were on our way to a modeling job at the time."

"A modeling job?"

"Yeah. I did that a lot as a little kid."

"You did?"

"Yeah. Before my mom married my dad, she was a casting director for a big studio. Lots of major brands would come to shoot there back then. This was in the late '70s, early '80s. Back before there were agencies outside of major markets like New York and LA."

"Go on," my supervisor said.

"So, my mom was in charge of casting for the studio. She actually started the careers of several folks who are still

50

Exegesis

modeling today. And she would book my dad all the time back then, too, and—"

"Wait. Your dad was a model, too?" she interrupted.

"Yeah. He did it for several years in New York. He was with Wilhelmina."

"Wilhelmina?"

"Yeah, sorry. I said that like you should know it. It's one of the major modeling agencies. I only know it because I heard it all the time when I was a kid. My mom would tell me about how handsome my dad was, and about how he could have been really famous, and about how they spent their first years of marriage with him in New York and her in North Carolina, with him modeling and her casting, and how he ended up coming home to settle down because it just didn't make sense for them to be apart like that."

"So, when you were in the car that day with your mom, you were going to a modeling job that your mom picked you for?"

I shook my head. "No. By that time she had quit her job to focus on raising me."

"What makes you think you're the reason she quit her job?"

"Because she told me so."

The supervisor looked at me, though she said nothing.

"So, yeah—she'd quit her job by then, but one of the models she'd found years earlier, a young woman she used to book a lot, had recently begun her own modeling agency, and it quickly became one of the biggest agencies in the Southeast. Still is. And by that time, I was on the scene, so I became kind of like the go-to child model for that agency."

PART TWO: WRITING

"And you were how old at this time?"

"I don't know. Like, three."

"But you said that you were eight in the story you're telling."

"Yeah, so?"

"So, you'd been modeling every day for five years?"

"Well, not *every* day. Not even most days. But I was doing it all the time. Many of my childhood memories are of hanging around at photography studios."

"That was probably a lot of money you were making," she said.

"Huh?"

"I mean, models get paid pretty well, right?"

"Yeah, usually. But I was just a kid, then. And it's not like I had a bank account."

"You mean you never saw any of that money? It wasn't saved or put into a trust fund or a savings account or anything like that?"

"No," I said, getting frustrated because she was missing the point. "All I'm saying is that when the song came on the radio that day and my mom said what she said, we were on our way to a modeling job. That's it. I honestly don't even know why I mentioned it."

"Well, clearly you have parents who were both very talented."

"Yeah," I said. "Before my mom became a casting director, she was a singer. She was really, really good. Like, amazingly good. She almost got signed by a big record label when she was younger, not long before she met my dad."

"So, both of your parents were once on their way to being famous—or, at least they both wanted to be?"

I shrugged. "Sort of, I guess."

52

Exegesis

"But years later your mom talked about that song and made you think that she had regrets about it all?"

I shook my head. "No. That song was about having regrets about marrying my dad, not about missing out on some kind of fame."

My supervisor's eyes got suddenly sad. "You don't think those two things are related, Austin?"

IF WE ARE BEING RESPONSIBLE and are engaging seriously and critically with the text, we should be spending at least two to three hours each week on sermon prep. I personally consult four different commentaries each week (sometimes more), and I print the Scripture in four different translations so that I can look at them side by side. Among the most critical questions I try to answer are:

- What is the sociohistorical context of this passage?
- What is the larger theology in which this passage is embedded?
- What biblical allusions or cross-references appear in (or could be applicable to) this passage?
- What have various scholars and pastors made of this passage throughout the centuries?
- What key words could prove fruitful if subjected to a Greek or Hebrew word study?

These questions are by no means exhaustive, nor are they meant to be prescriptive. I simply cite them as examples that I myself use in order to arrive at a deeper background knowledge of the passage at hand. That said, no matter what resources we use in our exegetical work and no matter what critical questions we put to them, what matters

PART TWO: WRITING

most is our ability to distill this overload of information into a few key points. Then, of equal importance is knowing how to insert these key points into the sermon in such a way that they will draw as little attention to themselves as possible—cooling the air without causing a distracting rumble.

THE THING ABOUT THOSE conversations with my CPE supervisor is that there was too much information to share. I didn't know how to talk about any of it without talking about all of it; and, what's more, I didn't at that point really understand any of it. I had not yet begun to process things and connect certain dots. So, I shared that one story—because it's the story that happened to come to mind when pressed that day—but I shied away from saying anything more.

There was so much about the man and the minister I was trying to become—and that *was* the point of these sessions, right? I didn't want to overwhelm our time together with an overload of details about my childhood and my formative years. I wanted to stay focused. I wanted to learn how to be a better caregiver. I didn't want to talk about the past; I wanted to prepare myself for the future.

ONCE WE HAVE COMPILED ALL the requisite information about our Scripture passage, it is helpful to list the items worthy of making it into the actual sermon. Make no mistake: *all* of this information is important, but all of it is not equally important for the point we're trying to make. So, make a list and then cross out the items that seem to be superfluous or beside the point. Likewise, cross out any items that would be too inflammatory or offensive for your congregation. Finally, cross out all items that you can still reference in the sermon without overtly naming them.

Exegesis

Bankruptcy. The night Dad shared the news with Mom. (How Mom fell into my arms like a helpless child. How I promised her it would all be okay. How I believed that.)

Dad calling from work to put a beer in the freezer. (My earliest memory?)

~~When Mom strangely took me to her old boyfriend's house when I was three. (When I asked her about it twenty-five years later and she replied: "You remember that?")~~

~~When Mom told me about how her old boyfriend used to call the house to talk to her and how much it would upset Dad. How Dad referred to him as "Mergers and Acquisitions" because the guy was so financially successful. (I was seven.)~~

~~How Mom used to make me practice smiling. Particularly in the car before we'd go to a modeling shoot. ("You're so handsome, Austin. But the way you're smiling right now makes you look like you smell something bad.")~~

How much Mom and Dad both loved me. How often they told me they loved me. How true it was. How much it meant to me. (How much it still means to me.)

~~How Mom used to subscribe to all the gossip magazines. How she talked about the celebrities like they were gods and goddesses.~~

~~How Mom used to tell me about other women thinking Dad was the most handsome person ever. How she'd light up when someone talked about how handsome he was. (How this suddenly began to stop~~

PART TWO: WRITING

~~once Dad hit his late forties.) (How this made~~
~~me feel pity, though I couldn't understand why.)~~

How proud of them I always was. Both of
them. (How proud of them I still am.)

~~How Mom used to tell me I'd one day be fa-~~
~~mous. ("You'll remember me then, right? Oh, I'm~~
~~so proud of you, baby!")~~

~~How Mom used to make me promise that she'd~~
~~always be my best girl. ("I'll always be your~~
~~best girl no matter what, right, sweetheart?")~~

~~How I learned to tell stories and make jokes~~
~~and be affable: at home, with larger family,~~
~~out in public. How this always eased tensions~~
~~between them and made everybody happy. (I'd~~
~~guess I was four or five?)~~

~~How Dad used to scream at me from the side-~~
~~lines of soccer games. ("Get your head in the~~
~~game, Austin!")~~

~~How Mom and Dad would both glow when I'd~~
~~score goals, hit game-winning shots, get my~~
~~name in the newspaper, etc. (Especially Dad.)~~

How happy it made me to make Dad happy.

~~How disappointed Mom was when I didn't get~~
~~voted best-looking in my senior class. How~~
~~she came up with various conspiracy theories~~
~~for why I didn't. (How I felt like I'd let~~
~~her down.)~~

~~How Mom told me . . .~~

~~How Mom told my sister (who then told me)~~
~~. . .~~

~~How I still carry that secret.~~

56

Exegesis

How I suddenly stopped drinking. (How I didn't make the connection for over a decade.)

~~Dad driving into that telephone pole and leaving the car at the scene. Telling me the next day that he'd seen a dog run out in the street. (This, after telling me the night before--while still drunk--that a car had swerved in front of him.)~~

Seeing Dad hide beer cans in the bushes and then confronting him about it.

~~Loaning Dad money and telling him that, with it, I had one request: that he stop drinking. How earnest he was as he promised he would stop. (How two days later, I saw him hiding his beers in the bushes.)~~

~~Dad getting his first DUI.~~

~~Dad getting his second DUI.~~

~~Going all the way to the beach to bail Dad out of jail. (The bail bondsman recognizing me from television and asking to take a picture with me. Mom beside me, momentarily comforted by this.)~~

~~Seeing Dad in that orange jumpsuit at his arraignment. (How I pretended like I needed to pee so Mom and Liz wouldn't see me cry but how I fell apart as soon as I got to the bathroom.)~~

~~How scared and pitiful Dad looked. How sad his eyes were.~~

~~That trip to check him into rehab. (All of those visits to see him. How high our hopes were.)~~

PART TWO: WRITING

How much alike Dad and I are.

How scared I am of it happening to me.

How Grandma was so ~~fanatical~~ disciplined about exercise and swimming. (~~Was this an addiction? A good one? Is this where it comes from for us?~~)

How committed Dad was to his faith. (How he used to read his Bible every night and how it always sat on his bedside table.)

How committed to faith Grandma was.

~~Seeing where Dad . . .~~

~~Seeing Dad's text from . . .~~

THE KEY IN THE EXEGESIS panel is to let the congregation sense the background information without realizing they are being presented with it—to insert it into a larger gloss on the Scripture in such a way that, if you were later to share a piece of background detail you chose not to use, they'd nonetheless see how it helped inform the sermon you wrote.

And that's it for the exegesis panel.

It is the part of the sermon that demands the most time, energy, and emotional engagement, but it's the part of the sermon that nonetheless needs to be the least conspicuous.

7

Story

The thing that makes Anne Lamott such a great essayist is her ability to tell a story. She uses her stories in service of important and profound truths, but the stories themselves are the heartbeat of her essays. If Fred Craddock once responded to criticisms that his sermons were too much story and too little sermon by saying that the stories *were* the sermon, then the same holds true for Lamott: her stories *are* her essays.

What makes Lamott particularly effective at this, though, is how effortlessly and how casually she tells her stories. How she weaves a story in and out of an essay and how seamlessly she puts down a story thread and then picks it back up. Her stories are at once captivating and simple, almost always more personal than plot-driven, and they have a way of conveying her greater point through the prism of her own life story.

THROUGH LAMOTT'S *TRAVELING MERCIES*, I learned how to couple the Coldplay panel with this next panel, the story panel—a panel that runs parallel to the Coldplay panel

PART TWO: WRITING

and, by extension, parallel to the sermon's thesis. Remember: at this point we haven't yet revealed the thesis. We have only begun to install the support panels, placing them in such a way that they will make the thesis appear in stark relief once we finally name it.

For this to work, the parallelism of (a) the Coldplay panel and (b) the story panel and (c) the thesis panel is absolutely vital. Even if we have an effective hook that piques the congregation's attention and a story that captivates the congregation and pulls them forward, if these panels don't mirror one another in such a way that, once the main idea is revealed, it is clear that these panels *were all the while conveying the thesis*, then this approach will be ineffective.

Thus, we might do well to momentarily switch our metaphor and picture these three panels as three parallel lines, all running in congruence with one another:

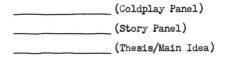

AFTER FINISHING REHAB, my dad took his sobriety seriously. He returned home apologetic for and ashamed of all that had happened, and he was sincerely committed to making amends and to abstaining from alcohol. It was a glorious stretch of time; it was as if someone long dead had come back to life. It felt like a resurrection had taken place, as if the stone had been rolled away and the guy who had once been my father had suddenly emerged from the tomb.

April and I had been married for a few years at this point, so the time my dad and I got to spend together

Story

during this period was more limited than it would have been if I were still single. I was now working as a high school English teacher rather than a freelance writer, which meant that I didn't have my days free to go to the gym with him like I used to. And it's not every newlywed's dream to spend her evenings watching sports and hearing her husband and her father-in-law argue about Duke versus North Carolina and gab about people they saw every day at the gym. So, my dad and I weren't together nearly as often during this period as we were in our heyday. Nonetheless, we were as close to one another during this period as at any time since he'd started drinking.

IT'S HARD TO OVERSTATE how many dreams I have quietly nurtured about fame, how many avenues I have imagined myself going down in hopes of becoming noteworthy in the eyes of an admiring public. Through high school I went back and forth in my imagination between three different paths to fame: modeling, soccer, and acting. At the time, I thought that each path was viable. By that point I had been featured in national ads for brands like Hanes and Wrangler and John Deere; I was being recruited by several Division I colleges to play soccer; and I was being invited to audition for then-popular television shows like *Dawson's Creek*, receiving praise from casting directors and being led to believe that my big break was just around the corner.

So, I'd lie in bed at night and imagine myself inhabiting each of these realities.

All these years later, I can still remember certain of these daydreams with utter clarity. In one of them, I am hanging out on-site with other young models, all of us

PART TWO: WRITING

fresh off an Abercrombie & Fitch shoot, and I'm laughing and joking with everyone about our upcoming bookings. The dream then flashes to me being back at home with my mom, telling her about Bruce Weber (the famous photographer) and about what it's really like behind the scenes of an Abercrombie shoot. In another dream I am playing for Boca Juniors, a professional soccer club in Buenos Aires (where my dad did most of his business); in the dream I score a goal and the Argentine crowd goes wild and lifts a banner with my name on it. As my team and I celebrate, I look to the stands where I see my dad and his Argentinian business partner, Ivan, jumping up and down and hugging one another. In yet another dream I am having dinner with (then-married) Brad Pitt and Jennifer Aniston on the back patio of their house, and I am asking them what it was like to experience fame and attention, and Jennifer says, "You'll soon find out for yourself."

I beg you: please don't resent the egotism of the young boy who was dreaming of such things; please don't hold entirely against him his massive privilege and the ease with which he could conjure such fictions.

Instead, please try to pity this boy, this naïve child who had no idea how out of his depth he was, or how empty he felt, or how scared he was—not to mention how unaware he was as to why such dreams felt so direly consequential to him in the first place.

Please try to pity him and empathize with him.

Because the truth is, that young boy *did* go to New York and LA, only to be turned away by every major modeling agency in both cities. And that young boy *did* go on to play Division I soccer, quitting after his junior year because he

Story

was not even in the starting lineup and because he realized he no longer even enjoyed playing. And that young boy *did* continue to audition for acting roles, finally landing a role on *One Tree Hill*, only to have his "recurring role" never actually "recur," ultimately being told by a major agent in Los Angeles that, if he were ever going to make it in the industry, he'd first have to prostitute himself on the city streets.

Yes, please try to pity him and have compassion for him, because I promise you: that young boy eventually *did* return home, utterly humbled, his eyes now open, better aware of his place in the world and the privilege from which he comes.

FOLKS STILL OFTEN ASK ME about how I ended up on *Survivor*, about how a small-town pastor like myself who today leads such a quiet and unglamorous life ever found himself on a show like that. And the simplest and most straightforward answer to that question is: through my sister, Elizabeth.

Among other such accolades, Elizabeth was once Miss Teen North Carolina; and while my family and I were at the 2004 Miss Teen USA pageant in Palm Springs, a casting agent from CBS approached me and asked if I would be interested in being on the show. The full story is of course longer and more involved than that, but that's essentially how it all began.

It was because of Elizabeth.

I'll never forget how crushed I was for Liz the night she did not win that Miss Teen USA pageant. I remember how, on the night before she'd left for Palm Springs, she and I had discussed how different things would be if she were to

63

PART TWO: WRITING

win, how she would become immediately famous and how exciting it would be for all of us to see her on the various morning shows the day after she'd won. She and I talked and joked that night about how we were always trying to one-up each other—her accomplishing one thing to gain fame, me accomplishing something to up the ante—and the two of us acknowledging that this could be *the* thing. How, if she won, she'd have truly arrived.

She cried so hard that night when she didn't win.

What surprised me then—and what took me years to understand—was that, once alone in my room that night, I cried even harder than she had.

HERE'S ANOTHER DAYDREAM I HAD back in those days. Between the time I learned I'd been cast for *Survivor* and the time I left to tape the show—which was a period of about two weeks—I used to imagine myself being announced the winner on live TV. In the dream I'd be sitting with the other (imagined) finalist, and Jeff Probst would be standing before us, and a live audience would be watching in breathless anticipation, and Jeff would pull that final name and say, "The winner of *Survivor Panama: Exile Island*—Austin!"

At this time my parents' finances were in bad shape, and though I didn't know just *how* bad, I could tell my dad was scared. Real scared. So much so that one day at the gym he joked that if I were to win the show, my winnings would be enough to shore things up for our family.

Thus, in the daydream, as Jeff announces me the winner, I hug the other finalist, and then—with the camera following me—I walk down to the audience, where my

Story

parents and sister are sitting in the front row, and I hug them and tell my dad that the money is his. All his. I shout over the loudness of the cheering crowd behind us that I'd done it all for him because he'd done so much for me. And in the dream my mom is crying, her face wet with tears, tears of pure joy.

Meanwhile, of equal interest for this story—and this is a detail of the daydream that I didn't note at the time—Liz is crying, too. Only her tears, I see now, didn't speak so much of joy as they did of relief and deliverance.

THE DAY I LEFT FOR *Survivor*, Liz hugged me at the airport and placed a letter in my hand. I read it on the plane and here's what it said:

"Dear Bubby,

" . . .

" . . .

" . . .

" . . . you've done it. What we've always wanted. You're going to be famous. I love you and I'm so proud of you."

SURVIVOR HAD COME AND GONE by the time my dad went to rehab. So too had the release of my first book. And while both of these things had indeed drawn some attention, soon enough they were just memories. What little money I had made from the show and the book was long gone, so I found myself teaching high school English in order to have a stable paycheck and dependable insurance.

When Dad got out of rehab, it was almost as if we could breathe again. Sure, teaching high school English was not

PART TWO: WRITING

glamorous, and sure, it kept me barely above the poverty line—but perhaps this quiet life was what we all needed. Liz was just out of college and teaching special education, and it seemed that perhaps all was in fact going to be okay.

AFTER SEVERAL MONTHS OF DAD'S sobriety, after I'd just begun to trust that things were indeed getting better, and that Dad himself *was* better, April and I had dinner with my parents at the home they were renting.

The following afternoon April pulled me aside and, with deep consternation on her face, said, "There's something I need to tell you."

Scared, I waited.

"I didn't know whether to say anything, because it's not really my place. But I think you need to know."

"What is it?"

"Last night, when I went upstairs to use the bathroom, your dad's toiletry kit was open on the back of the toilet."

"Yeah, so?" I said, willing her to get to the point.

"Austin, there was a bag of weed in it."

"A bag of *weed?*"

Defensively, she said, "You know I would never go through his stuff. It was just sitting there at the top. Like he'd just forgotten to hide it or put it away or something."

I could feel my body tingling, anger and sorrow and rage coursing through me, and I thanked her for telling me. I hugged her, and I assured her she'd done the right thing by telling me, and I dashed straight out to my car to head to their house. My mom had left that day to stay overnight with her sister, so I knew he'd be alone when I got there to confront him.

66

Story

What I didn't expect, though, was that I'd find him drunk and high, half asleep on the couch, empty beer cans littered beside him and a bag of marijuana on the coffee table.

"Dad!" I yelled, preparing myself to unleash the rage I felt.

In response, I heard a weak, sleepy response.

"Austin? That you, buddy?"

I watched him sit up and register everything that was going on—watched him look at the empty cans and then at the open bag and then, finally, at me. I saw how scared and empty and helpless he looked.

Then, as he walked toward me and tried to act as if nothing was going on, as if this were all completely normal, I felt the rage finally burst through. I began screaming profanities at him. I asked him why he was doing this, why he couldn't stop. Didn't he know what it was doing to everybody? Didn't he know how much it hurt? Didn't he know how much we needed him?

He listened to all of this, and he took it all in and he just looked at me all the while. He was standing so close to me I could see his heart beating. Then, finally, when I could scream no longer, he said to me—as sincerely as anyone has ever said anything to me—"I'm sorry, Son."

I screamed a few more times in response to this; mean and hateful things. Things I wish I could take back. But I couldn't pull myself together. And before I knew it, he was hugging me. He was pulling me in to him and continuing to say how sorry he was. And then, as he hugged me, the following words suddenly escaped my mouth—words utterly unexpected, bubbling up from a depth and a place I didn't know existed.

PART TWO: WRITING

"I'm so sorry I couldn't fix it," I cried. "I'm so sorry I couldn't fix it."

THE THING ABOUT THE STORY panel is that once we've placed it, we do well to turn immediately away from it, giving no indication of its bearing on the sermon's thesis. The sermon is best served if we instead leave the story hanging there—hanging long enough that, by the time we *do* finally reveal the main point, the congregation has already forgotten about the story. That way, once the point of the sermon has been made clear, the joy of connection comes upon the listener by surprise, the dopamine secreting, the congregation seeing in a flash how (a) the Coldplay panel and (b) the story panel and (c) the main idea have all the while been running parallel to one another, but how it took the revelation of the main point for the congruency to become visible.

8

Theology

I first discovered Frederick Buechner as a novelist, devouring *The Book of Bebb* and quickly going on to read the rest of his fiction. A few years later I began to read his nonfiction, and a few years after that I finally sat down with a collection of his sermons. It was only natural that I would feel a kinship with Buechner, seeing as his trajectory as a writer—from fiction to essays to sermons—mirrored my own. Buechner, like Lamott, is deeply personal with his essays, and he brings this same vulnerability to his sermons. Through little vignettes from his own life, Buechner is able to establish a theological undergirding to his work without drawing excessive attention to complex theological ideas. When I finally discovered Buechner-as-preacher—finding to my delight that his sermons bore the same literary mark as his essays and novels—I found not only a preacher I admired but a model for how to creatively embed theology in my own sermons.

MY EARLIEST MEMORIES OF CHURCH take place in a finished basement. This was my grandparents' basement, and

PART TWO: WRITING

people from the Jesus movement began flocking to it for worship in the late 1960s. My dad's father, a colonel in the air force, had undergone a dramatic conversion experience soon after his retirement, and he'd quickly become a pioneer in the (then) burgeoning home church movement. My grandpa was a very charismatic person—both personally and theologically—and people were drawn to him like moths to flame. By the time I arrived on the scene, the home church he and my grandma had launched in the late '60s had become a popular place of worship, and many young families had been worshiping together for over a decade. While there was no preaching here—scripted sermons and written prayers were discouraged in order to make space for the Spirit—it was a loving and peaceful environment, and when I think back on it, two principal memories emerge: how safe I felt in that place, and how much everyone admired my grandpa and jockeyed for his attention.

IT IS MISLEADING TO DESCRIBE my grandpa as a fundamentalist. He most certainly *was* a fundamentalist, but he was also very gentle, and most people do not think "gentle" when thinking of fundamentalists. He was dogmatic about theology and Scripture (like *all* fundamentalists), but he was also empathic concerning people's doubts and lived experiences. He was a man of conviction but also a man of kindness, and whether or not one agreed with him about matters of ultimate concern, everyone liked him and respected him.

I remember a Sunday morning as a child—I was probably four or five—when church had just ended and a group of adults were sitting around talking. My grandpa was hold-

Theology

ing court, and I was sitting in my dad's lap, and something was said that—who knows why—prompted me to speak up. I don't remember what I said, but no sooner had I said it than the adults gathered began to howl. One of them said, "That was pretty clever, young man. Looks like you're going to be just like your grandpa when you grow up."

THROUGH HIGH SCHOOL AND EARLY into college, I used to sit at my grandpa's feet in the afternoons and learn from him. He would pull out his thumb-worn Bible and instruct me in what he called "the Elementary Doctrines," a set of teachings he had drawn from Hebrews 5:12 and shared with other home church leaders as he traveled up and down the eastern seaboard. No matter what my grandpa happened to be teaching on, his core preoccupation was the power of the Holy Spirit, how we ought never to limit in our imaginations what the Spirit might be up to in the world. I revered my grandpa for both his personality and his perspective, his steady faith and his hopeful optimism, and I drank down to the dregs everything he ever shared with me.

NOT LONG AFTER MY DAD'S stint in rehab and his subsequent relapse, I left my job teaching high school English to enter seminary. I opted to attend a very progressive divinity school—by that time I had become more aware of the inequities and injustices of the world, and I wanted a theology that would inspire me to responsive action—but I was concerned about how my grandpa would feel about my decision. I knew that the theological education I would be receiving was in tension with many of his own beliefs, and I feared his disapproval. He was in failing health by

PART TWO: WRITING

this point, and I worried that my announcement might upset him.

"Grandpa?" I said, showing up to his house the day I told him.

"Aus, that you, Son?"

I walked into his room. He was no longer ambulatory, so I found him where I nearly always found him in those days: in his recliner, his Bible beside him.

"Hey, Grandpa," I said, hugging him.

"Have a seat," he said, motioning to my grandma's empty recliner just beside him. "What's on your mind?"

"Well," I said. "I've decided to go to divinity school."

"Oh, yeah?" he said.

I nodded.

"Where are you going to go?" he asked.

I told him, and then I waited for his response.

He sat quietly for a moment and considered. Then, looking back to me, he said, "Well, Son. Who knows what the Spirit might be up to?"

He gave me his blessing that day, and that was the last time my grandpa and I ever spoke of theology and Scripture. He died less than a year later.

ENTERING SEMINARY WAS LIKE FINDING a new home. Here were people who took seriously theological questions and were interested in the development of doctrine and the history of the Christian church. Moreover, here were people who were concerned about things like racism, economic inequality, environmental degradation, and a full range of sociopolitical and sociocultural questions I too was animated by. I threw myself into my studies, reading far

72

Theology

beyond the assigned readings and auditing courses I didn't even need for my degree. I felt like I'd entered heaven.

One of the things that surprised me, though, was how questions of orthodoxy seemed to be of secondary importance for many of my professors and classmates. The resurrection *may* have been a historical event, some said, but either way it was not central to Christian faith. And the kingdom of God *may* be an in-breaking reality, but even if not, the peaceable kingdom is potent enough as a symbol.

Such statements were unsettling for a young man who had spent untold hours learning "the Elementary Doctrines" from his fundamentalist grandpa, not to mention one who'd come of age during the boom of '90s evangelicalism. The resurrection of Jesus as *optional*? His return with the kingdom a *symbol*?

These professors and students were brilliant, though, and all these years later I still remember how patient and kind they were to me, how encouraging and affirming, and how I left seminary with a desire to please them and make them proud.

UNTIL SPENDING TIME WITH Buechner's sermons, I'd encountered few examples of preachers who could so effectively marry orthodoxy and social justice, and even fewer who could marry them in such a gentle, poetic way. Soon enough, I began trying to channel Buechner's style, not only literarily but theologically.

Years later, having now revisited a decade's worth of my old sermons, it is clear to me that, in those early years, I struggled to find Buechner's balance. In some of these

PART TWO: WRITING

old sermons—particularly the earliest ones—there is an overemphasis on *doing*. I make little connection in these sermons between the call to action and the resurrection of Jesus, and my tone is far more combative than suits my natural temperament.

Meanwhile, there are sermons from this period in which I place a great deal of emphasis on matters of belief while almost entirely neglecting calls for social action. Interestingly, here too one finds an aggressive tone, as if I am once again preaching *at* someone (albeit, clearly a different someone).

All through these vacillations—and I say "vacillations" because the process was not so much linear as it was back-and-forth, like homiletical schizophrenia—I was indeed trying to be poetic, trying to pay close attention to things like language and rhythm and cadence and imagery, but I seem to be doing it simply to appear literary, not in order to marry orthodoxy with biblical justice.

Unlike Buechner, I'd name-check several theologians in the same sermon—presumably to demonstrate that I'd read them—and I'd develop theological ideas that would utterly overwhelm the rest of the sermon (in one of these, I lay out every single step of Anselm's ontological argument).

Eventually, I'd come to balance these elements more evenly and effectively, learning to enrich the Coldplay panel, the exegesis panel, and the story panel by setting them alongside this theological panel, but it took a great deal of work and a lot of trial and error to find this balance. And while there are countless other creative ways to embed theology in a sermon—and each preacher's theology is necessarily going to be different—I champion the effect

Theology

of Buechner on my own sermons so as to make a much larger and far more critical point about sermon writing in general: One does not have to be combative as a preacher to be prophetic, and one does not have to shy away from social issues to remain orthodox. In fact, one never knows what the Spirit might do in the world if we will remain faithful to them both.

9

Thesis

It was not only Klosterman's use of misdirection that captivated my imagination all those years ago; it was also the way he came out and directly stated his main point. Rather than do what writers like Dillard, Lamott, and Buechner do, which is leave a reader to infer the point, Klosterman was on the nose with his thesis, often saying something as direct as, "Here's the thing: _____."

And then he'd say the thing.

I didn't understand right away why this resonated with me as strongly as it did, but I'd later see that it was because of a clever use of irony. Rather than make his reader work for the takeaway of what was already a creative and sophisticated essay, he—after all that artistry—would simply give it away for free.

When I discovered Dave Eggers's *A Heartbreaking Work of Staggering Genius*, I more fully understood what writers like Klosterman were up to—Eggers, too, used irony by directly naming the (typically) unnamed part, which made one's revelation of the main idea even more haunting, as it therefore echoed long after the point had been made.

Thesis

THE PREACHER HADDON ROBINSON WRITES that "narratives are most effective when the audience hears the story and arrives at the speaker's ideas without the ideas being stated directly."

I respectfully disagree.

If a preacher has placed the various panels of his or her sermon parallel to one another, being careful to keep hidden how they are quietly working in harmony, then the revelation of the main idea is not only surprising but also illuminating, as each panel suddenly magnifies the sermon's message, much like a stained-glass window suddenly catching the day's strongest light.

IT IS VITAL THAT the main idea be kept short and sweet; for once stated, its effect will only be dulled by restatement or elaboration.

SO, HERE'S THE THING: I thought I had run away from something I had been unable to fix, but then I unwittingly spent an entire decade trying to fix it through writing sermons.

10

Resolution

I was a high school student when *Pulp Fiction* was released, and like most everyone at the time, I was transfixed by it. The way Tarantino told the story in such a jarring fashion, introducing one aspect of the plot and then shifting to another (and then another, and then another) without drawing any direct connection between them all—this approach to filmmaking was altogether new to me. About halfway through the film I remember thinking that Tarantino was attempting some sort of dada aesthetic, that we'd be entertained by a bunch of unrelated vignettes that, when placed side by side, would merely represent the absurdity of all things. I was pleasantly surprised, therefore, when the film coalesced around a central moment and, from there, began to pull the threads together, the viewer suddenly seeing how each one had all the while been central to the story Tarantino was telling. This Pulp Fiction effect is what a sermon's resolution should aim for: to pull together the sermon's various threads.

Or, perhaps better—to place a frame around the parallel panels.

Resolution

THIS SHOULD LOOK SOMETHING like this:

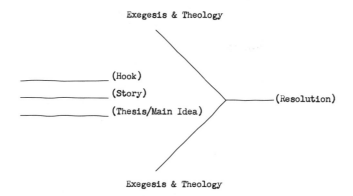

LIKE THE MAIN IDEA, the resolution should be kept brief, reintroducing the various threads that have been presented (and left hanging), but should not be drawn out or further interpreted. Instead, here is the moment of the sermon in which the joy of association should reach its climax, as the congregant now sits with the echo of the main idea—which, remember, has just been named—and infers the connection between it and everything that has been left hanging.

I WAS WALKING TO LUNCH with a colleague a few years ago, reflecting on life and ministry, when I said something that stopped me short. "It may be that my whole ministry has been an attempt to go back to the beginning and understand what happened."

This thought had never occurred to me before, and I was unsettled by hearing myself speak it aloud.

PART TWO: WRITING

"To go back and understand what happened," he asked, "or to go back and fix it?"

I walked in silence for a few beats as I considered his question.

"Is there a difference?" I finally said.

I see now that there is indeed a difference—for one can try to understand something without deluding himself or herself into thinking that, through better understanding it, it will be fixed. I see clearly now that, through the hundreds of sermons I have preached, I have been doing more than trying to understand everything.

When striking that combative tone early on, I was at once preaching *at* my family and *at* those who would judge and condemn them. Meanwhile, I was trying to find my way back to that finished basement, that place where I felt like those who surrounded me—my dad and my mom, my grandpa and my grandma—fully understood me, and where I fully understood them. The place where *they saw the child*, and the place where the child felt he could rest safely in his father's lap.

I see now how preoccupied my sermons have been with warnings against the temptations of fame and money, and how April's steadying presence has informed so many of my admonitions against false optimism and religious escapism. I see, too, how a reliance on the Holy Spirit has remained central to everything I have ever preached, even when I didn't think I was preaching on the Holy Spirit at all.

Most significantly, though, I see now how every sermon I have ever preached—and how every spiritual thing I have ever said—has been in part an effort to recall my family to who we really are, and an attempt to make my whole family proud.

All of this, I see now, has been a heartbreaking work of staggering genius—not genius in the sense of innate brilliance, but genius in the sense of deriving from my innermost self: a work of misdirection so cleverly applied that the truth of what I was doing was hidden even from me.

In short: I see now that the practice of sermon writing is indeed a gift of self-discovery and that, through it, some of us find that—after all of our running—we've never really left home at all.

PART THREE

REVISION

11

Perspective

Once we have a complete sermon draft, the first thing we must do—before we get into other, more substantive editorial work—is read our initial document and discern whether we have presented our thesis in an evenhanded and credible way. We do well to ask ourselves preliminary questions like:

- Have I made sweeping generalizations?
- Have I overargued my point?
- Have I taken into account my own biases?
- Have I considered other viable points of view?
- Have I sufficiently justified my claims?

One of the things a congregation most appreciates about a sermon is a preacher's willingness to speak with conviction while simultaneously recognizing that his or her own perspective is necessarily limited by background and circumstance.

Case in point: last week I preached a sermon about the decadence of our society and the shallowness of our preoccupations—ultimately in service of claiming that our

85

PART THREE: REVISION

distractedness prevents us from seeing the ever-present movement of God in the world—and my first draft featured this sentence:

> But we as twenty-first-century American Christians are in such thrall to our smart phones and our YouTube channels, and so mired in our dependence on streaming video and Amazon Prime, and so desirous of the latest news about new restaurants or new boutiques, that we can't possibly see or hear the Holy Spirit because—as Neil Postman puts it—we're so busy "amusing ourselves to death."

When I began to read my initial draft, looking for cases of my own limitation and bias, I quickly ran up against this sentence. Not because of the content—I stand by the claim—but because of the overgeneralized "we."

Yes, the congregation *I* happen to serve, which is entirely middle to upper-middle class, is indeed fairly represented by this "we." However, as the sentence stands, it suggests that *all* twenty-first-century American Christians are preoccupied with such things, and that is patently untrue. Millions of Christians are scraping by to make ends meet, and many more live on sidewalks or under overpasses. These brothers and sisters in Christ are not obsessing over new restaurants to try or the allure of overnight shipping; they are focused on where to get their next meal and where to sleep at night. Thus, I amended the sentence to say:

> But we as twenty-first-century American Christians—
> at least, *those of us who are financially secure, upwardly*

Perspective

mobile twenty-first-century American Christians—are in such thrall to our smart phones and our YouTube channels . . .

It is a small change, but it makes a real difference. Life, faith, and reality are complex, and congregants want to know that their pastor understands that.

ONE OF THE BEST THINGS I did while in divinity school was take several courses in the philosophy department, and a habit I learned while writing my philosophy papers has become one of my most dependable tools for editing sermons.

Unlike theology or history papers, and certainly unlike novel and essay writing, philosophy papers demand that one not only present one's own case—and present evidence *for* one's own case—but that one also anticipate and rebut all possible arguments *against* one's case.

I hated doing this, and it made for some incredibly tedious and ponderous papers, but it has become a key discipline for me in sermon editing. Which is to say, after reading each sermon draft, I list all possible rebuttals. I also flag at least ten places in the sermon that are ripe for those rebuttals, because this causes me to peruse the draft more carefully and to read with a greater self-awareness.

1. I haven't said anything about how patient and forgiving Dad and Mom have always been with me--and how much I gave them to forgive.
2. I have made myself sound too passive, too

PART THREE: REVISION

much the victim, as if I weren't the one asking to play soccer, and asking to change schools to increase my visibility as a recruit, and asking for unlimited soccer equipment and attire; as if I weren't the one setting up meetings with agencies in Atlanta and New York and LA; as if I weren't the one begging Dad to buy my friends and me beer as an underage kid; as if I weren't the one who absolutely loved having Dad come to the bars with us when we were old enough to start going.

3. I haven't mentioned how Mom and Dad essentially kept me afloat through my midtwenties, letting me live with them so I could continue to pursue my dreams of literary success. (Note: if I'm going to write of financial hardship and its effects on our family, I better acknowledge how much financial ease there was most of the time—and particularly how much I benefited from it.)

4. I haven't mentioned how affectionate Dad and Mom so often were with one another. Perhaps I have made it sound like there was a coldness to their marriage, or as if they were openly hostile with one another, which was never the case.

5. I have dwelt only on the negative ramifications of Mom and Dad pouring their lives into Liz and me while not talking enough about the positives:

Perspective

a. How close we all always were, and how much fun we had (note: How many people can say this? As a pastor, I know better than anyone how rare this is).

b. How physically safe we always were (note: not only did we live in a big, warm house in the most desirable neighborhood in town, we also knew our parents to be gentle and kind).

c. How funny they were and how at ease we always felt with one another (note: I remember long car trips where we'd laugh together with a warmth and familiarity that few people ever experience).

d. How encouraged and affirmed they made us both feel (note: they never laughed at a dream or hope or idea either of us ever had; they supported every single one).

e. How provided for we always were (note: I didn't have to pay a dime for undergraduate school, something I am still reaping the benefits for while the majority of my peers are servicing exorbitant student-loan debt. And this is not to mention all the clothes, gadgets, cars, etc., through the years).

6. I haven't talked about how much trouble I caused as a teenager and young adult;

PART THREE: REVISION

how reckless I was; how dishonorably I treated a great many people; how much this grieved and wearied both Dad and Mom—particularly Mom.

7. I haven't acknowledged how necessarily limited my knowledge is of Mom's and Dad's lives; their childhoods; their marriage; what went on behind the scenes all those years; how necessarily clueless I am about their deepest fears and wounds and regrets.

8. Am I narrating this story as if it is the story instead of my story? (If so, I must take care that I make it clear that I know everything is far more complicated than I am presenting it to be, lest I look naïve or, worse, ungrateful.)

9. I haven't mentioned that Liz would likely tell this whole story differently. And I haven't mentioned that while I have distanced myself from the whole situation, she not only remains embedded in it but shoulders even more burden because I left. Nor have I mentioned that I fear she resents me for it and thinks that I have given up on our family, and that I have never broached this with her because it hurts too much to talk about it and because my biggest regret about all of it is feeling like I let her down and failed to protect her.

10. I haven't pointed out that I somehow believe that, even after people read all of

90

Perspective

```
this, Dad and Mom will not only forgive
me but will still be proud of me (note:
that such a thing would even seem possi-
ble says something about how fiercely and
unconditionally they have loved me all of
my life--because how absurd is it to think
such a thing?).
```

WE DO NOT NEED to incorporate in the sermon all the potential rebuttals, but we *do* need to include the key ones. Moreover, the final draft must clearly communicate that we are aware that our own perspective is limited: that while we believe wholeheartedly in our message, we likewise know that we—for now—see through a glass dimly. Sermons preached from a posture of certainty will almost always fail to reach twenty-first-century listeners where they are and achieve the desired effect, but sermons preached from a posture of humble conviction stand a fighting chance.

12

Tension

In *A Secular Age*, Charles Taylor describes life in the twenty-first century as "cross-pressured," as a reality in which one can never be fully at home in either religious faith *or* doubt. According to Taylor, the staunchest atheist has haunting encounters that raise anew the question "but what *if?*," and the most committed believer has moments of harrowing uncertainty. This is the primary reason why twenty-first-century congregations appreciate sermons that acknowledge the preacher's situatedness and limitation, because congregants hear in such sermons their own cross-pressured predicament.

Therefore, when we revise our first draft, we must note places where we have been overly dogmatic *and* places where we have not made clear enough how deeply we believe in what we are proclaiming.

Here's an example from a sermon I preached a few weeks ago. In my first draft, I wrote this:

> The fact that the resurrection happened means much more than that the second member of the Godhead

Tension

rose from the dead; it means that our own humanity has been brought through death and is risen with Jesus in an all-new creation.

As central to my theology as this statement is, I have put it too dogmatically here. The *fact* of the resurrection? According to whom? Proven how?

If I had preached the sermon without revising this sentence, two things would have happened: (1) those who don't currently accept a historical resurrection—of which we have several at my church—would have tuned me out, and (2) those who *do* accept a historical resurrection would not have been confronted anew with the scandal and the glory of its proclamation.

Thus, I edited the sentence to say:

If the resurrection actually happened—which I absolutely believe it did—then it means much more than that the second member of the Godhead rose from the dead. If the resurrection happened, then it means that our own humanity has been brought through death and is risen with Jesus in an all-new creation.

If Charles Taylor is right—and I believe he is—then those listening to us each Sunday are caught somewhere between the *if* and the *then*, somewhere between doubt and belief. It is our job as preachers not to sidestep this reality through fideism or dogmatism but to honor it through faithful conviction.

ONE DAY WHEN MY DAD took me to climb trees at the Quaker church, I got about halfway up my favorite tree,

PART THREE: REVISION

higher than I'd ever been before, and I looked down to make sure he was watching.

"Do you see me, Dad?" I called.

"Yes," he said. "You're doing it, buddy!"

My chest swelled with pride. "Do you love me?"

Beaming up at me, he said, "Son, you're the best thing that has ever happened to me."

ANOTHER CROSS-PRESSURE we live with as twenty-first-century preachers is an ever-present tension between competing ideologies. The people to whom we preach are daily inundated with propaganda that masquerades as news and by hostilities that masquerade as activism. They are being subtly formed to listen for ideological signifiers, even in places where they don't exist.

In *Prius or Pickup*, political scientists Marc Hetherington and Jonathan Weiler explain that, given the shallow, sound-bite culture in which we live, the average person now reduces the complexity of reality to the simplicity of signifiers.

Mention listening to NPR? *Liberal.*

Reference eating at Cracker Barrel? *Conservative.*

Use the word "oppression"? *Liberal.*

Speak positively of "tradition"? *Conservative.*

This is the climate we preachers inhabit, and we must be cognizant of how often our congregants impose meaning on certain words and references. Most don't even realize they are doing this—such is the subtle work of propaganda and formation—but this only increases the pressure on us as preachers, for a parishioner who hears a signifier that "others" him or her will begin to tune us out, often without even knowing why.

Tension

Therefore, if our primary concern is proclaiming the gospel of the crucified and risen Jesus—which it should be—then we must neutralize these cross-pressures so that those listening will *continue* to listen. This does not mean eliminating all words and references that could potentially serve as signifiers (this would be nearly impossible) but balancing such words and references in a fair and evenhanded way.

Case in point: In the first draft of a recent sermon I cited an article from the *New York Times* and referenced a landmark in San Francisco while not including any counterbalancing signifiers. Thus, I found places in the draft to seamlessly weave in other signifiers to ensure that no listeners would unconsciously tune me out.

Thus, in a sentence that originally said:

While we were in our car on the way to Greenville last weekend, Julianna said to me . . .

I edited it to say:

While we were in our Tahoe on the way to Greenville last weekend, Julianna said to me . . .

And then, in a sentence that originally said:

So, here we are without one plea.

I edited it to say:

So, like at an old-fashioned Billy Graham revival, here we are without one plea.

PART THREE: REVISION

Jonathan Haidt demonstrates in *The Righteous Mind* that 90 percent of our opinions are determined in advance of conscious thought. Logic, reason, and persuasion have an important place in human processing—why else would we be preaching if not—but studies show that we respond with our emotions and then work backward to justify our initial reactions. Haidt refers to our gut as our "elephant" and to our conscious cognition as our "rider," saying that once our elephant leans in one direction, it is difficult for our rider to steer the elephant another way.

This being the case, we do well as preachers to address our sermons to our congregations' elephants as much as to their riders. And, in a cross-pressured moment like the one in which we live, the most effective way to do this is by paying careful attention to whether our signifiers are properly balanced.

WHEN WE FINALLY STAGED an intervention for my dad, I felt deeply ambivalent about what we were doing. I knew by this point how much I wished he would stop drinking, but I also felt he had justifiable reasons *to* drink. As much as I loved my mom, I could clearly see how difficult it was for him to be married to her. And as much as I appreciated all he had done for me, I knew he could have lived a different and better life had it not *been* for me.

So, as we sat in a circle at his office, waiting for him in ambush, my heart was racing. What would he say? What would *I* say?

The shock on his face as he walked through the door was harrowing and pitiful. He quickly realized what was happening and grew defensive. My uncle put his arm around

Tension

him and walked him slowly toward our circle. My uncle said we were all there because we loved him and wanted to talk to him.

Reluctantly, my dad took a seat.

My grandpa went first, assuring my dad how much he loved him and how proud of him he was, but then telling him that his drinking was out of hand. My grandpa said he understood that my mom had put my dad through a lot, that he knew the strain in their marriage had been significant, and that he understood why he would be driven to drink. Nevertheless, my grandpa said, these things couldn't be solved through alcohol.

My uncle then picked up the same line, telling my dad how problematic his drinking had become while acknowledging that he understood why he had turned to drinking to begin with.

Then my dad's business partner repeated the same line.

Then my dad's longtime friend repeated the same line.

Then my grandma repeated the same line.

And on and on.

All the while I sat quietly listening, torn. I adored my mom, and I hated that she was having to listen to all this, but I also thought it was essentially true, so I didn't know what to say or do. At the time, it didn't occur to me how unfair it was that everyone at the intervention was from my dad's family or were friends of my dad; how unfair it was that my mom didn't have anyone there, except for Elizabeth, to plead her own side of this emotionally volatile and deeply complex situation.

Finally, I spoke up, and though I regret it now, I too repeated a version of the same line others had taken, saying

PART THREE: REVISION

that I wished my dad would stop drinking but that I loved him and felt like I understood why he did it. In short, I too gave him a pass.

When it was all over, with everyone crying, we hugged and made peace and left with hopeful hearts.

TWO DAYS LATER, I SAW my dad hiding beer bottles in the bushes again.

TWO WEEKS AFTER THAT, I WATCHED my dad calmly tell my mother that she had spent far too much money decorating his office, saying that as much as he appreciated it, they could not afford it. He asked her to please take most of it back.

In response to this my mother exploded, tearfully lamenting that my dad was ungrateful for what she'd done and saying that she clearly couldn't do anything right. She bolted out of the room and ran up the stairs, leaving my dad staring blankly and helplessly.

At me.

AS PREACHERS IN A SECULAR AGE, we can never escape the various cross-pressures of our moment, and our work as editors therefore must manage the conflict and hold the tension in proper balance.

13

Audience

Once we have attended to our personal limitations and the cross-pressures that surround us, we move on to our audience. Who are we preaching *to*? Where in the sermon are we making this clear? Are we preaching to a general audience or to *our* congregation—the flesh-and-blood folks sitting before us each Sunday?

Another thing I've found through rereading my earliest sermons is how general my audience seems to have been. Which is to say, nothing in these early sermons suggests they were preached to the members of First Baptist Church of Corbin, Kentucky; instead, these early sermons could have been preached to anyone, anywhere.

I once heard Winn Collier say that the particularity of Port William is what makes Wendell Berry's fiction work; no matter how gifted Berry is as a writer, it is the integrity of the specific, the people and the location of Port William, that draws readers to his fiction.

When hearing this, I immediately thought of a line from *Hannah Coulter*, where Berry writes that people nowadays are in a hurry to get to "some other place," which means they will ultimately end up in "no place."

PART THREE: REVISION

This can easily happen to preachers: we can be so eager to preach to everyone that we end up preaching to no one; so driven by the desire to increase our "reach" that we reach right past the very people we've been called to lead. (Particularly now that livestreaming and podcasting are so easy.)

Therefore, we do well in our first editorial pass to look for places where we've overgeneralized our audience and to make certain that our message is being aimed at *these* people, in *this* place.

HERE'S AN EASY EXAMPLE of what I mean. In a sermon from 2016, I say this:

> The other day I was with my daughter, Ada, and we went to a restaurant downtown called Travis's Café.

On the surface, this seems like an innocuous sentence. But I had already been at this church for two years; my congregation was 150 people—*max*—in a town of 7,800; and there were—*maybe*—eight restaurants downtown.

The point being: everyone in the sanctuary that morning knew who Ada was; I didn't have to add "my daughter." And everyone knew very well what (and where) Travis's Café was; they'd all been eating there much longer than I had.

Thus, it is abundantly clear all these years later that I was preaching to an imagined audience—to a general "crowd" versus a particular "congregation."

HAPPILY, I CAME ACROSS a sermon from 2021 that *also* included a story about Ada, but in this sermon, I simply said:

100

Audience

Ada and I were in the car on the way to Concord the other day, and she said something to me that I won't soon forget.

Such changes seem minor—the mere deletion of the words "my daughter" and the assumption that my entire audience knows that "Concord" is a local elementary school—but changes such as these reveal a great deal about the intentionality and the pastoral care of the preacher.

HERE IS A MORE significant example.

Early in my ministry I was struck by how different groups of people would approach me after a service to commend me on a sermon. I would hear from members of a certain group and then weeks would go by—sometimes months—without another word.

Around the time that I started to pick up on this pattern, I stumbled upon *Theological Worlds* by William Paul Jones. Jones makes the case that all of us are born with a dominant theological language; or, as Jones puts it, we inhabit a certain theological *world*. There are five of these worlds, and all of us resonate (at least slightly) with each of the five. However, each person has one *primary* world, one language in which the person most clearly hears his or her ultimate concern being named and engaged with.

The principal concern of each world is:

World One: A search for ultimate meaning
World Two: The reality of injustice in the world
World Three: The desire to become more fully oneself
World Four: The consciousness of sin and guilt
World Five: The inevitability of struggle and hardship

PART THREE: REVISION

While Jones's typology is far more sophisticated than this thumbnail sketch allows for, this is sufficient to highlight that our sermons should recognize that there are particular people *within* our particular congregations. Which is to say, even if we are preaching to "our" people (and not to a general audience), still, *our* people inhabit different theological worlds, each of them hearing the gospel most clearly when proclaimed in their own native language.

When a group would approach me about a sermon, it was because I was preaching in their primary language. Then, when I'd preach from a different world—speak, that is, in a different theological language—the first group would go silent and I'd hear from a different group.

Ever since encountering *Theological Worlds*, I have become conscientious about preaching to all five theological worlds in a roughly even manner. This has been enormously helpful because, until I became aware of this typology, I would preach the vast majority of my sermons out of my own world, speaking in my own native theological tongue.

Today, in the same way that I look carefully for places in which I have been overly general about my audience, I likewise pay close attention to whether I am being evenhanded in my articulation of these theological worlds—and if I have not been, I make a note to aim upcoming sermons at worlds that have not gotten enough recent attention.

IF WE ARE ADDRESSING our words to a general audience, our messages will necessarily become generic; which means that, in trying to reach a broader audience, we will diminish the sermon's impact on all who happen to hear it, even

Audience

the general audience we are trying to reach. Ironically, it is when we aim our words at a very specific audience—at *our* congregation; at *these* people—that the sermon begins to take on a wider appeal.

THUS FAR I HAVE ONLY talked about my ambitions as an athlete and an entertainer; I have scarcely mentioned my ambitions as a writer. Perhaps this is because my failure to achieve these ambitions was the most painful failure of them all. Suffice it to say that after fifteen years of dogged pursuit; after having been promised fame and fortune by the then-publishing person of the year; after having been promised even more by one of the industry's leading literary agents; and after having landed a deal with the biggest religion editor in the business, I watched the whole dream disintegrate in a poof.

This whole fifteen-year saga is a long and painful story for me, but the upshot is this: I used to fantasize about being on best-seller lists and moving in esteemed literary circles, about making a fortune through publishing and reaching as wide an audience as possible—but all of that went away the moment when, at what was supposed to be the climax of this fifteen-year pursuit, my dream editor and dream publisher rejected my proposal for a second book.

There's much more to this story, but that's the broad outline. April and I were weeks away from our wedding at the time, I needed a dependable income, and my energy to sustain the dream was finally gone. I began teaching high school English a month later, and I put away all hopes and dreams of literary success.

PART THREE: REVISION

Now, a lifetime later, as a pastor content with sermon writing as my primary mode of writing, the words you are reading are aimed at the smallest audience possible: myself.

For as Winn Collier said and as Wendell Berry has spent half a century making clear, what makes our words work as writers is our commitment to particularity; otherwise, we will find ourselves writing for everyone while reaching no one.

Trust me, I know.

14

Style

For well over half a century, writers have been citing William Strunk and E. B. White's *The Elements of Style* as the bible for writers. What Strunk and White achieved in terms of clarity, elegance, and simplicity is remarkable, and all writers do well to own a copy. Perhaps what is most helpful about *The Elements of Style*, though, is how the book identifies an element of style, justifies the rule for usage, cites an example, provides historical antecedents, and does all of this in (max) half a page per stylistic item.

THE THING ABOUT SERMON WRITING is that, when it comes to elements of style, it is up to the preacher to define his or her own stylistic cues—because the congregation only hears what the preacher *says*. Or, better yet: the congregation only hears how the preacher delivers the words they are hearing.

Depending upon grammatical style—that is, upon the cues one sees on the page—one can preach the exact same words while conveying entirely different messages.

PART THREE: REVISION

So here, then, is the whole point as this pertains to preaching: the way one chooses to format and punctuate a manuscript—in other words, the elements of style that one employs—ultimately determines how effectively he or she will deliver a sermon.

HERE ARE SOME of my own stylistic rules, each of which helps clarify (in the preaching moment) not only what I am *trying* to say but how I *need* to say it for my words to convey their true intent. Thus, what follows are examples of how my sermon text actually looks *on the page* as I prepare to preach.

1. RULE: Use em dashes to embed ancillary or clarifying claims in the middle of a point, and fret not about overusing this rhetorical device.
   ANTECEDENT: Dave Eggers's <u>A Heartbreaking Work of Staggering Genius</u>.
   EXPLANATION: Setting off subthoughts with em dashes is more effective than setting them off with commas or parentheses. This is because the effect of an em dash is abrupt, and it therefore draws more attention to what is being communicated.
   EXAMPLE: "Thus, the disciples beheld Jesus-- beheld this <u>same</u> Jesus, this Jesus whom they walked with and talked with and called by name on the near side of his crucifixion--in glorified, human form."
2. RULE: Use parentheses to cite a follow-up

106

Style

point within an already strong and otherwise finished phrase or sentence. Use parentheses more sparingly than em dashes, though, as parentheses can become distracting if overused.

> ANTECEDENT: Chuck Klosterman's Sex, Drugs, and Cocoa Puffs; Killing Yourself to Live; and Fargo Rock City.

> EXPLANATION: Sometimes it is helpful to add an afterthought to a phrase or sentence, allowing the afterthought to further magnify the point being made. That said, the parentheses should have the effect of lowering the register of the phrase or sentence, as if cueing one to speak in a slightly less declarative voice.

> EXAMPLE: "'So, come unto me, all you who are weary and heavy laden,' Jesus said (not only to his disciples but to the entire crowd that had followed them), 'and I will give you rest.'"

3. RULE: Use semicolons to conjoin two complete sentences or to enumerate items in an exceedingly long list (particularly if that list includes commas).

> ANTECEDENT: John Irving, in all novels but particularly in A Prayer for Owen Meany (in which he extols the beauty of a properly used semicolon).

> EXPLANATION: While it is helpful for cadence and pacing not to develop overly

PART THREE: REVISION

long sentences--which is almost inevita-
ble for any sentence that would require a
semicolon--the occasional long sentence,
if existing within a sermon of otherwise
shorter sentences, can draw powerful attention to itself. <u>Such sentences are
most effective if surrounded by shorter,
more metrical couplets (or tercets) on
either side.</u>

EXAMPLE:

"We do well to hope:

"We have no choice <u>but</u> to hope--

"For, the coming Kingdom of God is not
    purely about the future and is not
    purely about internal belief; in-
    stead, if we really <u>do</u> believe in
    the future coming of God's Kingdom,
    we will inevitably begin to live and
    move and have our being <u>now</u> as if the
    Kingdom has already arrived.

"So, let us not grow weary in doing what
    is right:

"Let us not turn from the problems of
    this world:

"Instead, let us turn <u>toward</u> our God-
    given responsibility of addressing
    them today."

4. RULE: Use colons to break up a sentence
into several distinct lines when the sentence includes a list with three or more
long phrases.

Style

ANTECEDENT: Unknown.

EXPLANATION: Breaking the list into shorter pieces helps with pacing, giving the congregation a better chance of following the point we are making.

EXAMPLE:

And thus, Jesus is saying here, when you want me to be abrasive, I am going to be gentle:

When you want me to be dominant, I am going to be peaceable:

When you want me to take advantage of my power, I am going to surrender it willingly:

When you want me to take no captives, I am going to set the captives free.

5. RULE: Use adverbs as sparingly as possible.

ANTECEDENT: Annie Dillard, Pilgrim at Tinker Creek and The Writing Life.

EXPLANATION: While adverbs can add clarity and emotion to a sentence, adverbs can also overcrowd the sentence and--worse-- cheapen the sentence by making it emotionally dependent on the adverb.

EXAMPLE: "~~Suddenly,~~ Jesus turned to his disciples and ~~angrily~~ said, 'Those who are ashamed of me and my way, of them will the Son of Man be ashamed when he returns again in glory.'"

6. RULE: Use italics to emphasize key words in a sentence.

PART THREE: REVISION

ANTECEDENT: Anne Lamott (for italicizing
  prepositions) and Klosterman (for italicizing key words).

EXPLANATION: When preaching, it is very helpful to know which parts of a sentence to
  draw attention to--or, put differently:
  it is very helpful to know where to place
  the sentence's emphasis so as to honor the
  rhythm of the cadence. (Often this falls on
  a preposition, though by no means always).

EXAMPLE: "And thus, this Lenten season, it
  is important that we <u>recognize</u> we have
  cheapened Christian discipleship, that
  we repent <u>of</u> it, and that we commit ourselves more closely to the way of <u>Jesus</u>."

THIS LIST ABOVE IS by no means exhaustive, but it does
capture aspects that are of key importance to me and to
my weekly delivery. I adhere to each of these rules closely,
because I have found over the years that, if I don't pay close
enough attention to how I want to say something—and to
how the words appear on the page so that I will, in fact, say
it that way—then I will unintentionally preach a different
message (that is, I will be heard in a way contrary to my true
intent), even though I am saying the exact same words.

MEANWHILE, HERE ARE SOME OTHER stylistic rules I have
graciously inherited and that I strive to live by. Rules that, like
the ones above, can convey two entirely different messages
depending upon how one delivers and receives them.

Style

1. RULE: Forgive quickly.
    ANTECEDENT: Dad, Mom, Grandpa, Grandma.
    EXPLANATION: Forgiving others is not only a
        charitable thing to do, it also unburdens
        you of anger and resentment you might
        otherwise carry around forever.
    ALTERNATIVE MESSAGE: When something painful
        happens, sublimate it and pretend like
        it never actually happened.
    ALTERNATIVE EXPLANATION: This helps you to
        live as if everything is fine, and, over
        time, allows you to believe it really is.
2. RULE: Be hopeful and optimistic.
    ANTECEDENT: Dad, Grandpa.
    EXPLANATION: In a world in which hard-
        ship, pain, and struggle are inevita-
        ble, there is also much that is beau-
        tiful and good. One's life is therefore
        enriched by remembering that goodness
        and beauty can always follow something
        tragic and painful.
    ALTERNATIVE MESSAGE: Look forward to a
        future event, convincing yourself that
        this hoped-for thing will absolutely
        take place.
    ALTERNATIVE EXPLANATION: This helps you to
        quiet all anxiety and fear and despair
        in the present by transferring all uncon-
        scious energy toward an imagined future.
3. RULE: Don't be afraid of your feelings or re-
    luctant to show your emotions.

PART THREE: REVISION

ANTECEDENT: Mom.

EXPLANATION: It is unhealthy to repress one's emotions, and demonstrating how we feel helps others to better know us and love us.

ALTERNATIVE MESSAGE: Seek out emotional music, film, literature, etc., so as to enjoy a good cry or to wallow in a hyperemotional experience.

ALTERNATIVE EXPLANATION: By purging yourself of emotion via manufactured media, you can release unwanted feelings without having to acknowledge the pain from which these emotions are actually welling.

4. RULE: Follow your passions.

ANTECEDENT: Grandma, Dad, Mom.

EXPLANATION: Nothing is more onerous than going through life doing things you don't like doing, so try as best you can to find things you enjoy. Such hobbies lend brightness to the darker parts of lived experience.

ALTERNATIVE MESSAGE: Dwell compulsively on something; it doesn't matter what.

ALTERNATIVE EXPLANATION: This gives you something to focus all your attention on so as not to have to focus attention on things less desirable.

5. RULE: Be gentle and peaceable.

ANTECEDENT: Grandpa, Dad, Mom.

EXPLANATION: Harshness and combativeness

Style

are not only unbecoming, they are coun-
terproductive in forming relationships
and accomplishing tasks. Gentleness and
peaceability, on the other hand, always
calm situations and draw people together.
ALTERNATIVE MESSAGE: Never show anger or
unhappiness to others.
ALTERNATIVE EXPLANATION: This makes people
more agreeable and endears people to you.

6. RULE: Be considerate of others.
ANTECEDENT: Grandpa, Dad, Mom.
EXPLANATION: The world does not revolve
around any one individual; therefore,
remember the feelings of others.
ALTERNATIVE MESSAGE: Try to please as many
people as you possibly can.
ALTERNATIVE EXPLANATION: This makes people like you, but more importantly, it
ensures that people are not mad at or
unhappy with you.

7. RULE: Always be willing to lend a helping
hand.
ANTECEDENT: Grandpa, Dad.
EXPLANATION: You never know how your willingness to help people will make the
difference in whatever they happen to be
going through.
ALTERNATIVE MESSAGE: Try to fix anyone who
is broken.
ALTERNATIVE EXPLANATION: This enables you
to overlook how broken you, yourself,

PART THREE: REVISION

really are and enables you to turn something that is a weakness into something
that seems (to you) heroic.

THE BENEFIT OF A GUIDE like *The Elements of Style* is
that, through it, one better understands rules of engagement that, like in life, could have been otherwise but that,
through repetitive use, have hardened into a definite form.
Thus, per consulting Strunk and White, one is better able
to recognize the reason for preexisting rules and better prepared to implement (or amend) them with utmost care and
scrupulosity, lest one's best intentions be misrepresented
or misheard.

15

Cuts

In apologizing for the length of a letter he'd written to a friend, Mark Twain apocryphally remarked, "I'm sorry this letter is so short; if I'd had more time, it would have been shorter." I think of this remark every time I sit down to edit a sermon, because no matter the length of our initial draft, the sermon can always be—and always *should* be—shorter.

That said, making cuts to our work can be painful. Typically, because what most needs to be cut is what we are proudest of. Stephen King calls this "killing our darlings"—"darlings" because of how precious these particular words usually are to us.

In my case, this most often takes place in the theology panel, because I have a tendency in my initial drafts to ignore Tom Long's advice about not exposing the congregation to the rumbling of the HVAC. Thus, I have countless times despaired over cutting a seven-hundred-word expatiation on, say, Paul Tillich's doctrine of God or Irenaeus's notion of soul formation. I remember spending over an hour one afternoon trying to convince myself that I could

PART THREE: REVISION

keep an entire section about Jürgen Moltmann's distinction between *futurum* and *adventus*, even though the sermon was only tangentially about biblical conceptions of time.

Studies show that the average duration for which a speaker can retain a listener's attention is about twenty minutes, which gives us a good and helpful benchmark to aim for (incidentally, this usually translates to about 2,200 words—at least for me).

Beyond this pragmatic reason for brevity, though, concision is an art, and exercising it demonstrates respect for the craft, as it acknowledges that sermon writing is something holy and worthy of care.

IN MY SECOND RECURRING DREAM, my dad has just lost his job, his drinking has just reached its zenith, he has just shown up hungover to a soccer game, and my friends are laughing about this on the sideline.

Suddenly, my coach—with ninety seconds left in a tied match—calls me off the bench to enter the game for the first time. Rather than pop up and run to midfield to await the official's signal to enter, I stand up and say to my coach, "Are you really going to disrespect me by putting me in *now?*"

My coach's face shows shock as I say this, and he simply turns away from me and calls someone else into the game. As he does, I look back to where my dad is standing behind the bench, where I know he has just watched this happen, and I see him give me a fist pump, as if to affirm me for what I've just done.

Though a recurring dream, this is a true story; and though it happened more than a quarter-century ago, I relive it in my sleep every few months.

Cuts

HERE'S WHY I TELL YOU about this dream.

That soccer game took place on a Saturday, and the following Monday my coach called me into his office to discipline me. He began by telling me that I'd be unable to dress or to travel with the team for the next two games. Then, easing his demeanor and assuming a gentleness that I found discomfiting, he said to me, "But what I really want to talk about is why it happened."

I stared at him.

"Something like this is really unlike you," he said.

I shrugged.

"I know things are tough at home right now with your dad losing his job, and I was wondering—"

Surprising myself, I cut him off. "This has nothing to do with my dad. If you need to suspend me, fine. But leave my dad out of this."

My coach sat silently for a few beats, and I saw pain in his face.

"Fair enough," he finally said. "We'll see you at practice in two weeks."

I quit soccer one month later, and I have not played a single day since.

YEARS LATER, WHEN MY MOM and my sister could no longer handle my dad's drinking, when he had already had a few wrecks and had already embarrassed them in public one too many times, they begged me to go with them to an Al-Anon meeting. I was uncomfortable with the idea, but I agreed to accompany them because I didn't want to let them down.

The meeting was held in a nondescript room at a small Presbyterian church, and we sat in a circle while people

PART THREE: REVISION

began to share about loved ones' addictions. Soon enough, Mom and Liz were talking, saying things about how awful Dad's drinking was, about how sad it made them, about how mad they were, about how it was like we'd lost him as a husband and a father. They were crying and choking up, and these strangers were all the while encouraging them, saying that it was okay, telling them to let it all out.

I listened as they aired these things out, and I could feel myself raging inside.

Finally, after Mom and Liz were done talking, the leader asked if I'd like to say anything, and I shook my head no—but then I began to speak anyway, my voice quivering, saying that I wasn't mad at Dad, saying that I loved him, saying that, yeah, he drank some but so what, that I loved him and could never be mad at him. I said that he'd been a good father to me and that he'd given up a lot for us and that everyone needed to recognize that.

When we left that night, a stranger slipped me a note. It was written on a napkin: "One day your anger will catch up with you. When it does, call me."

Under that, he left his phone number.

That, too, was over a quarter-century ago. I still have that napkin, though I never did make that call.

STEPHEN KING WRITES THAT AS much as we love our darlings, we must eventually kill them. Which is to say, once our first draft has been finished, and once we have begun the work of revision, if we are to be serious preachers, we must face and eliminate those parts of our sermon that are hampering or obfuscating the transformative truth we are pursuing.

Cuts

SO, THEN. HERE GOES: My dad is an alcoholic, and he always will be. And despite the complexity of everything else involved, his alcohol abuse is *the* central element in my family's decades-long breakdown. I am indeed angry about it, and I have spent the vast majority of my life saying (and believing) otherwise.

And here's why I have: Because I am so much like him. Because I see in him the same scared, sweet-natured little boy that hides deep within myself, the same little boy that only ever wanted the best for everyone, that only ever wanted to make everyone around him happy. All my life I have wanted to honor and defend this little boy for his goodness and purity.

In short, I defend him because I *see* him. Because I see the child *in* him. The child in both of us.

And I defend him because I ache for both of these children.

IN *ON WRITING WELL*, William Zinsser claims that most first drafts can be cut by over 50 percent without losing anything necessary, and I assure you that well over 50 percent of the book you're holding lies on the cutting-room floor. If the final product therefore feels short, please understand that if I'd had more time, it would have been even shorter, but that, as it turns out, I had to spend most of my time killing my most precious darling.

16

Arrangement

We begin each sermon draft with an idea of what order things should go in, of what will happen in our proclamation and of what sections we should prioritize. Seldom, though, do the needs of our final draft fit our preconceived ideas.

Instead, we usually find ourselves having to move things around, having to put, say, the theology panel closer to the top while moving the story panel to the end; or having to eliminate the story panel altogether while using our exegesis panel as the hook.

More often than not, our panels quickly cease to be separate things and begin to merge together, our exegesis happening *in* a story, or our theological development serving *as* our resolution.

In short, each sermon has its own integrity and works best via its own inner logic. The hardest and most demanding part of our editorial work, therefore, is discerning how best to fit everything together to make the strongest final draft possible.

Arrangement

FOR THE FIRST THREE YEARS of our marriage, April and I spent countless hours responding to crises and breakdowns within my family, processing new developments and grieving the recurrent nature of the various addictions and emotional needs. This was of course hard on me, but what I didn't appreciate at the time was how much harder it was on April. She loved my parents, very much in fact, but she had not married them—she had married me.

Eventually, we became pregnant with Ada, and when it came time for Ada to be born, she arrived eight weeks early. Premature as she was, we were told by doctors that she would have to spend at least a month in NICU, maybe longer.

The hospital was forty-five minutes from our house. So, needing (and wanting) to remain nearby, we found a room at the local Ronald McDonald House and prepared ourselves for a lengthy stay.

Unfortunately, though, we had two dogs at home that we couldn't bring with us, that we couldn't afford to board, and that we had nowhere else to send. My mom and my dad had finally separated by this point, and neither of their respective places was conducive for animals, so I said to April, "I'm sure my dad would be willing to go by the house each day to feed them and let them out."

April, cradling Ada in her arms, took on a pained expression and said, "We have a baby now, Austin. If he's going to do that, he can't go to our house to get drunk and smoke weed."

She paused.

"I'm sorry," she said. "But he just can't."

PART THREE: REVISION

The clarity in that moment was tremendous, the realization of how out of order my priorities had all this time been. So, I moved closer to April, I put my arm around her and gently cupped my palm around my newborn daughter's head, and I responded, "No, Sweetheart. You're right. He can't."

FROM THAT AFTERNOON ON, my resolve to withdraw from the intractable crisis and to attend to the needs of my own growing family only continued to strengthen, the pull I felt from my painful past slightly diminishing with each new day. Two years later, we were called to a church in southeast Kentucky, and as our moving truck crossed the Tennessee line, I knew in my soul that the reprioritization process was now complete.

WHEN PUTTING THE FINISHING TOUCHES on our drafts, it is perfectly natural to grieve the loss of our original idea; that is to say, the framework out of which we first began to write. That said, if we will remain attentive to the arrangement the Spirit is calling us to, our sermons will shine with greater truth and deeper integrity on that account.

17

Critique

In the early years of our marriage, long before children came into the picture, April and I used to stay up late into the night reading to one another. The first book we ever read together was Jodi Picoult's *My Sister's Keeper*, and I remember the experience vividly because I recall thinking to myself, as April would pause to reflect on certain passages, *how did I ever get so lucky?*

She'd do that often, I'd soon find out: pause in the narrative to reflect on something she'd just read. She'd then look to me and ask, "What do you think?"

Through those early years we read all sorts of books together; Anne Lamott's *Grace Eventually* and Cormac McCarthy's *The Road* come to mind, as do Kelly Corrigan's *The Middle Place* and Lois Lowry's *The Giver*. But the book we read together that I remember most fondly—not to mention with the most clarity—was C. S. Lewis's *Till We Have Faces*.

We spent an entire weekend reading that book together, beginning on a Friday afternoon and finishing on a Sunday evening. It was early autumn, and depending on the time

PART THREE: REVISION

of day, we'd move from the porch to the couch to the bed, stopping only for meals and for bathroom breaks. Both of us were transfixed by the book—not so much by the story as by its profundity and depth.

All these years later I remember how, late in the novel, there was a line that April paused to reflect upon:

> To say the thing you really mean, the whole of it, nothing more or less or other than what you really mean, that is the whole art and joy of words.

"What do you think?" she then asked me.

That was almost two decades ago, but that moment—and that line—has stuck with me ever since.

AFTER FINISHING A ROUGH DRAFT and a round (or two) of revisions, we do well to preach the sermon to a trusted friend or colleague and receive constructive criticism. We should choose someone we can ask, "What do you think?" and receive helpful feedback and insight.

Every Thursday afternoon, after my sermon has gone through the necessary revisions, after my limitations and my audience have been considered and the necessary words and passages cut out, I preach it to my three pastoral colleagues, James Bennett, Lucy Cauthen, and Anna Kate Stephenson.

They respond with feedback on what is working and what is not working, on what parts I should eliminate and what parts I should further flesh out.

Invariably, this criticism makes my sermon stronger and tighter—not only because of their keen editorial skill

Critique

but because these three know my theology, my intentions, my heart, and my voice as well as anyone in the world.

This is the key to receiving the right kind of critique: we must only entrust our work to a select few, those whom we can be vulnerable with and who know us as well as—or perhaps even better than—we know ourselves.

STEPHEN KING REFERS TO a trusted reader as one's "Ideal Reader," and he says that every writer must have an Ideal Reader, because a writer needs someone who can lovingly point out the hardest things of all about a work-in-progress and do so in a way that one can hear the criticism and receive it.

Fortunately, I have an Ideal Reader, and my Ideal Reader lovingly pointed out to me the hardest thing of all about the present book. "I think you give your father too much credit and your mother not enough," my Ideal Reader said to me. "And I just wonder, why is that?"

Sometimes we can kill our darlings on our own, but other times we need an Ideal Reader to point out where our darlings are hiding.

IN *THE DEEPEST BELONGING*, after reflecting on the numerous years she'd spent grieving the breakdown of her family of origin, pastor Kara Root finds herself looking at her own family, at her husband, Andy, and their two children, and she writes, "Quite suddenly I realized that my family's collapse was no longer my life's most defining experience."

I thought about that line a few nights ago while helping Ada with her homework. She had been assigned a chapter from Judy Blume's *Freckle Juice* and was reading it aloud to me, and I was lying beside her, marveling at how quickly she

PART THREE: REVISION

had grown up. Suddenly, like her mother long before her, she paused to reflect on a sentence she had just read:

I'd hate to see you without them. They're part of you.

As Ada paused, my mind traveled back to those long-ago nights when April and I would lie in bed reading to one another, every now and then putting our books down to dream about what might become of our lives, of what we might do and who we might become.

"Do you think there will be a baby here between us one day?" April asked me on one of those nights.

It was the first time either of us had ever broached the topic of children.

"I don't know," I said, after a long pause. "I hope so."

Two decades later, our oldest daughter lying beside me, her younger sister in bed beside us, their two brothers fast asleep down the hall, I began to reflect on how much has changed in our lives since that conversation. On how much I have changed; on how much April has changed; on how much *we* have changed.

I'd hate to see you without them. They're part of you.

These children, I suddenly realized; this woman; our family; *us*: I'd hate to see myself without them. They're part of me. They *are* me. My life has meaning and clarity and purpose because of them. They are the defining story of my life.

The meditative pause in Ada's reading didn't last long, and soon she was back at it; and soon enough, I was back

Critique

out of my reverie. But as Ada finished the chapter, and as she put the book down and asked me, in precisely the same way her mother used to ask me long ago, "So, what do you think?," I responded to her by saying the whole of what I really meant, nothing more or less or other.

"I think," I answered, "that this family is the best thing that has ever happened to me."

18

Punctuation

Every sermon, like every life, is a kind of prayer.
Therefore, end each one with "Amen."

EPILOGUE

Final Draft

I once heard an old preacher, riffing on the story of David and Goliath, say that every sermon is like a little rock, a powerful force when aimed with faithful precision. I have thought about that image a lot over the course of writing this book, turning over a decade's worth of rocks and interrogating how faithfully I've aimed them. Despite their many flaws, each of these sermons displays a struggle to say something meaningful and true, and what strikes me now, all these years later, is that what seems to me most meaningful and true in them is not what I thought when first writing them. This is the great mystery of writing—that we don't really know what we are trying to say when we begin, and that it's only after we're finished that we discover the truth we have all the while been pursuing.

"When you write," Annie Dillard says, "you lay out a line of words. . . . You write it all, discovering it at the end of the line."

ONCE WE HAVE FINISHED our revisions on Friday, we do well to leave off opening the document again until Sunday

EPILOGUE

morning. By this point, the words are too familiar to us, too close, for us to do anything further constructive. We now need a period of time to distance ourselves from the words so that we can encounter them fresh on Sunday morning.

IN MY THIRD AND FINAL recurring dream, I am in a car that has just lost control and is suddenly hydroplaning. I turn the wheel feverishly trying to stop the car from spinning, but always to no avail. Each time, I awake terrified just before my vehicle crashes into the corner of a brick house.

JOHN STOTT WRITES THAT EVERY sermon should include all four elements of the overarching biblical story: creation, fall, redemption, and consummation. Thus, when we arrive at church on Sunday morning, prepared to polish the draft and shape it into its final form, we must make certain that we are indeed covering the full narrative arc, sounding notes of original blessedness and present brokenness, of unexpected redemption and glorious transformation. In that way, every sermon—like every life—should be filled with wonder and pain, struggle and hope, crushing despair and astonishing surprise.

WHEN I WAS DROPPED as a client by the then-publishing person of the year, he sent me an email that said, "Your words will one day make a mark."

A lifetime later, what I find astonishing is that after letting go of my literary dreams only to receive them back as an unexpected grace, tiny fragments of six different unpublished projects—each unrelated and written across the span of fifteen years—have become central elements of the

Final Draft

present book. None of these fragments felt, when I wrote them, like important pieces of the work I was pursuing; and none of these fragments were in my mind when I sat down to write what you are holding.

And so it is that we write by faith and not by sight, trusting that our words will one day make a mark, never knowing how they might one day be transfigured.

MUCH IS MADE ABOUT ORIGINALITY in art, about the burden and necessity of creating work that is distinct and unique, and preachers are by no means immune from the anxiety of influence. No one wants to be considered derivative; everyone wants to be thought of as visionary and cutting-edge. But the truth is, if we are being faithful to the call, and if we are being honest with ourselves, we know we will never be able to escape the influence of others. Nor should we want to. For we are products of everyone who has ever loved us, hurt us, taught us, and inspired us, and our words are influenced by the writers and preachers and poets and prophets we have admired and wrestled with and thought about and looked up to. This is inescapable, and it is something that should be celebrated, not lamented.

BY DISTANCING OURSELVES from our sermon on Saturday, we can more clearly see on Sunday where redemption and transformation are shining through in what we've written, and also where we need to make these climactic elements of the story line even clearer.

This, then, is the final revision of all: we must finally draw into focus the unexpected redemption and the glorious transformation that await the children of God.

EPILOGUE

LAST SUMMER, MY DAD six months sober, he and I were sitting together on the balcony of a beach condo, both of us quietly reading our Bibles. It had been nearly thirty years since I had last seen my dad read Scripture, and the Bible he was reading was the same one that lay by his bed each night when I was a child. I had been shocked to see him pull it out of his bag when he arrived, just as I had been shocked to learn how long he'd been sober.

After a stretch of silence, he looked up to me and said, "Your grandpa would sure like to see us like this, wouldn't he?"

"He'd be very happy," I responded.

My dad sat quietly thinking, then he said, "I'm proud of you, Son."

To which I replied, "I'm proud of you too, Dad."

I HAVE FOUND THROUGH YEARS of heartbreak and struggle that we cannot fix other people—that despite what Coldplay says about lights guiding us home and igniting our bones, still, try as we might, we will never be able to fix the brokenness of one another's lives.

And I hate Coldplay for saying otherwise.

JUST AS IMPORTANTLY, I HAVE FOUND through years of writing and rewriting, editing and revising, that we will never be able to fix a sermon. Which is to say, no matter how much time we spend on a sermon and no matter how masterful we become at the craft, still, we will never write a perfect sermon. Instead, our sermons will inevitably show blemishes and shortcomings, will contain things that could have been better said and things that would have been better left unsaid.

Final Draft

So, here's the thing: at a certain point in the process, we must stop trying to control our sermons and must learn instead to trust the Spirit of God, for who knows what mark our insufficient and soon-forgotten words might make when the transformative wind of an eternal tomorrow sweeps them up and carries them away?

THE GREAT CHRISTIAN HOPE is that, through a divine mystery, that which is excellent and true in this world will be pulled forward into the world to come. That whatever in this world is gold will not only survive the refining fire of Kingdom Come but will in fact be the raw material out of which the kingdom will be built.

On this side of that eternal tomorrow, it is hard for us to distinguish what is dross from what is pure; what is wood, hay, and stubble from what is solid gold and everlasting.

But the Spirit knows, and it is the Spirit that gives life.

Therefore, we keep writing. Word by word. Line by line. Knowing that at the end of the line we will discover what all the writing has been about.

ON THE NIGHT I WAS dropped by my publisher, the night my literary dream finally died, I found myself pulling Norman Maclean's *A River Runs through It* off of my shelf and, for reasons I didn't then understand, reading the entire book in one sitting and being comforted by the closing words:

> Eventually all things merge into one, and a river runs through it. The river was cut by the world's great flood and runs over rocks from the basement of time. On some of the rocks are timeless raindrops. Under the

EPILOGUE

rocks are the words, and some of the words are theirs.

I am haunted by waters.

ONE DAY ALL OF US as children of God will awake to a transformed reality, the scars we bear in the present shining with transfiguration. All the good traits we have inherited and passed on will remain; all our weaknesses and short-comings will have been purged.

Eventually, all things *will* merge into one—the final draft.

Meanwhile, here in our brokenness, we ache at the memory of our original glory and we long for the day of our coming redemption. As we groan, we aim our rocks one by one, praying they will reach their target and trusting that, for the many that don't, a time is appointed under heaven for gathering them in.

Until then, under the rocks are our words.

And some of our words are theirs.

For we are haunted by others.

Always and inescapably, we are haunted by others. And thanks be to God that we are.

AMEN.

Postscript

Yesterday afternoon I stood underneath a Japanese cherry tree in full bloom, watching Witt climb higher than I had ever seen him climb. When finally he began to climb back down, he suddenly slipped and found himself dangling from a low-hanging branch. Panicked, he called out to me.

"Dad, help!"

Standing nearby, surveying how close to the ground he actually was, I said, "Just let go, buddy. It will be all right."

"I can't," he screamed.

"Yes," I said. "You can. I promise. Just let go."

I watched him as he flailed around for a few moments, his little legs kicking at the air.

Finally, trusting my words, he released his grip and fell safely to the ground, where he landed in a bed of daffodils that had just opened themselves to the warmth and welcome of spring.